About Island Press

Island Press is the only nonprofit organization in the United States whose principal purpose is the publication of books on environmental issues and natural resource management. We provide solutions-oriented information to professionals, public officials, business and community leaders, and concerned citizens who are shaping responses to environmental problems.

In 2001, Island Press celebrates its seventeenth anniversary as the leading provider of timely and practical books that take a multidisciplinary approach to critical environmental concerns. Our growing list of titles reflects our commitment to bringing the best of an expanding body of literature to the environmental community throughout North America and the world.

Support for Island Press is provided by The Bullitt Foundation, The Mary Flagler Cary Charitable Trust, The Nathan Cummings Foundation, Geraldine R. Dodge Foundation, Doris Duke Charitable Foundation, The Charles Engelhard Foundation, The Ford Foundation, The George Gund Foundation, The Vira I. Heinz Endowment, The William and Flora Hewlett Foundation, W. Alton Jones Foundation, The John D. and Catherine T. MacArthur Foundation, The Andrew W. Mellon Foundation, The Charles Stewart Mott Foundation, The Curtis and Edith Munson Foundation, National Fish and Wildlife Foundation, The New-Land Foundation, Oak Foundation, The Overbrook Foundation, The David and Lucile Packard Foundation, The Pew Charitable Trusts, Rockefeller Brothers Fund, The Winslow Foundation, and other generous donors.

Who Owns the Sky?

Also by Peter Barnes

Pawns: The Plight of the Citizen-Soldier

The People's Land: A Primer on Land Reform in the United States

Who Owns the Sky?

Our Common Assets and the Future of Capitalism

Peter Barnes

ISLAND PRESS
Washington • Covelo • London

Library of Congress Cataloging-in-Publication Data
Barnes, Peter, 1942–
   Who owns the sky? : our common assets and the future of capitalism / Peter Barnes.
         p.   cm.
Includes bibliographical references and index.
      ISBN 1-55963-854-0 (cloth : alk. paper) — ISBN 1-55963-855-9 (pbk. : alk. paper)
      1. Air quality management—Economic aspects—United States. 2. Space debris—Economic aspects—United States. 3. Airspace (Law)—United States. 4. Climatic changes—Government policy—United States. 5. Global environmental change—Government policy—United States. 6. Capitalism—United States. I. Title.
   HC110.A4 B297 2000
   363.739'2—dc21
                                                          2001001681

British Library Cataloguing-in-Publication Data available.
Printed on recycled, acid-free paper ♲

Manufactured in the United States of America
10 9 8 7 6 5 4 3 2 1

For Zachary, Eli, and Jackie

Acknowledgments

Gratitude is heaven itself.
—William Blake

I owe my fascination with the inner workings of capitalism to my father, Leo Barnes, an economist who specialized in stock market analysis. When I was growing up in New York City, he wrote a book called *Your Investments,* a popular guide to investing. The book included dozens of charts and tables with headings such as "100 Companies That Have Never Missed a Dividend" and "Historic Price-Earnings Ratios." For many years my father updated the book for new editions and hired me to recompute his tables. This meant pouring over microscopic numbers in Standard & Poor's and Moody's reports, hand-entering data onto big sheets of accounting paper, and literally crunching numbers on what was then a state-of-the-art Friden mechanical calculator. (It took a good sixty seconds of noisy gear-gnashing—or so it seemed—for the machine to perform a single act of long division.)

Thanks to my father, the names IBM, General Electric, and Procter & Gamble, and the statistics associated with them, were as familiar to me as those of the Knicks and Yankees. Though I had only the vaguest idea of what these corporations did, I understood that millions of grown-ups made guesses about their future ratios, and that some of them got rich by doing this.

As I grew older, my father frequently encouraged me to *think* like an economist: to understand ratios, trends and cycles, and the impacts of public policies. And he shared with me his lifelong yen for philosophy—for asking big questions and digging for deep answers. It's thus he who, long ago, planted the seeds of this book.

My mother, Regina Barnes, enriched the soil. A passionate and punctilious teacher of English, she was both adored and feared by her students at the High School of Music and Art. As her son, I could understand why. At home, she radiated a love of poetics (and theatrics, and puns) with as much intensity as she applied to pointing out my every grammatical lapse. She was also an outspoken union activist and FDR liberal. Her hand and heart can be felt thoughout these pages.

The thinking that led to the actual writing of this book began in the 1990s, when I was president of Working Assets. We were in the telecommunications business, so I became familiar with auctions of the broadcast spectrum to cellular companies. Later I learned about similar auctions of sulfur emission permits, and arranged for Working Assets' customers—by rounding up their phone bills to the nearest dollar—to purchase and retire about $50,000 worth of such emission permits, thereby keeping our air a tiny bit cleaner. To my colleagues at Working Assets—especially to Laura Scher and Michael Kieschnick—I say thanks.

After leaving Working Assets, I found homes for my musings at Redefining Progress and the Corporation for Enterprise Development. I thank my colleagues there for contributing greatly to the evolution of this book—especially Bob Friedman, Rafe Pomerance, Brian Dabson, Jonathan Rowe, Ted Halstead, Richard Norgaard, Martha Phillips, Joanne Kliejunas, Bill Schweke, Marc Wetherhorn, Helen Payne Watt, Gabriel Wishik, Gary Wolff, Jeff Hamond, and Cliff Cobb. None of them, of course, should be blamed for the form my ideas have finally taken.

Among the talented writers who passed through the Mesa Refuge, a writer's retreat I co-founded in Northern California, many were sources of help and inspiration. I'm grateful in particular to David Bollier, Ross

Gelbspan, Tom Athanasiou, Terry Tempest Williams, Meredith Maran, Dean Baker, Edgar Cahn, Diane Dumanoski, Michael Sherraden, Mary Clark, Robert Frenay, Curt Menke, and Jeff Gates.

Wendy Wallbridge, a great personal coach, helped me focus and move forward with clarity and resolve. Others whose advice I sought (though often ignored) were Roger Hickey, Bob Kuttner, Hans Riemer, John Richard, Thilo Bode, Frank Muller, Ray Kopp, Gerald Torres, John Echeverria, Annie Petsonk, Daniel Dudek, John Passacantando, Ken Cook, Phil Clapp, Denis Hayes, Wolfgang Sachs, Aubrey Meyer, Sunita Narain, Lee Lane, Bill Curry, A. Denny Ellerman, Richard Parker, David Olsen, Derek Shearer, Tim Hargrave, John Knox, Michael Lerner, David Morris, Mike Noble, Jane Perkins, Jim Boyce, and Marc Breslow.

Todd Baldwin, my editor at Island Press, understood this book immediately and gracefully spirited it into print. Anna Lappé added artistic flair. Jean Bernstein, my mother-in-law, served as meticulous copy editor and #1 fan. And I'd be remiss if I didn't mention others whose achievements inspired me over the years: E. F. Schumacher, John Kenneth Galbraith, Henry George, James Lovelock, Herman Daly, and Jay Hammond, governor of Alaska.

I'm also indebted to the funders who supported the Sky Trust initiative: the Ford, Gerbode, Turner, W. Alton Jones, Wallace Global, Rasmussen, Tides, Surdna, Energy, and Jenifer Altman Foundations, as well as Rena Shulsky and the New York Community Trust. Their generosity helped move a novel idea into the political marketplace.

My extraordinary extended family—Leyna Bernstein, Pam Miller, Zachary Barnes Miller, Eli Barnes, Jackie Mauro, and Thea Mauro—sustained me and put up with my absences throughout the writing process. To them I am eternally grateful. It takes a village to produce a book as well as a child.

My deep gratitude also goes to the creator of our miraculous universe, of which the earth and its inhabitants are small but precious parts. I'm not a religious person in the conventional sense, but I share the awe and humility toward the creation that most religions teach. The least we can do as we pass through our brief physical existence is to protect this inherited handiwork from our own ignorant depredations. That task begins, but doesn't end, with gratitude.

One final note. This book is part of a burgeoning citizens' movement to define the sky as a shared dividend-paying asset. If you'd like up-to-date information on this effort, log on to <www.skyowners.org>.

PETER BARNES
Point Reyes Station, California

Vocabulary

Vocabulary is everything when explaining new concepts. In this book I employ a number of phrases that are either not in common use or are frequently understood to mean something other than what I intend. The following list of key words and phrases will therefore help you avoid some confusion.

Alaska Permanent Fund, n. A trust established by the people of Alaska to invest and distribute the state's oil income to all Alaskans equally

algorithm, n. A simple formula, often repeated, which drives a complex system

anthropogenic, adj. Caused by humans, as in *anthropogenic climate change*

asset, n. Anything owned that has value; a thing that generates income

assetize, v. To convert an unowned commons into an asset held by a trust

beneficial owner, n. The individual or set of individuals that receives income from an asset

beneficiary, n. The individual or set of individuals that receives income from a trust

biodiversity, n. The richness of nature, as seen in the quantity and distribution of species

biosphere, n. The region on, above, and below the surface of the earth in which all known life exists

cap-and-trade system, n. A market-based pollution reduction system in which a limited number of pollution permits are created, distributed, and traded

capitalism, n. The market-driven system of production and trade that currently prevails in most of the world

CFCs, n. Abbreviation for chlorofluorocarbons, a family of human-made compounds that are good refrigerants, aerosols, and solvents but also destroy stratospheric ozone

common asset, n. A valuable shared asset, such as the atmosphere

commoner, n. An ordinary citizen; in Britain, anyone not part of the gentry

commons, n. Historically, a pasture or woodland used collectively by commoners; more broadly, a natural or social asset that is neither privately nor state-owned

common sector, n. The portion of a country's economy that is based on common assets

corporation, n. A self-perpetuating legal entity, chartered by the state and owned by stockholders, that is allowed to engage in business

cost of goods sold, n. The direct costs paid by businesses to produce their goods and services

demand, n. In economics, the money buyers are willing to pay for goods available in the market

derivative, n. A modern financial instrument, such as a pork belly future, whose value derives from another asset; typically used for hedging and speculating

dividend, n. A distribution of earnings to business owners

ecosystem, n. A natural system that sustains life (*see also* system) *equity,* n. Fairness; in business, the owner's stake

externality, n. A cost that is *not* part of a business's cost of goods sold; a cost borne by others

fiduciary responsibility, n. The legal obligation of a trustee to act on behalf of a beneficiary

Gaia, n. Ancient Greek goddess of the earth; the name given to a scientific theory that holds that the biosphere and living organisms act in concert to maintain the conditions necessary for life

Genuine Progress Indicator (GPI), n. An economic yardstick that tracks changes in the well-being of a population

global warming, n. The warming of the earth's climate due to increased concentrations of greenhouse gases in the atmosphere

governor, n. An automatic mechanical device that limits the speed of an engine

greenhouse effect, n. The natural process by which certain gases in the atmosphere let the sun's heat *in* but not *out*

greenhouse gases, n. Trace gases in the atmosphere that trap heat; the most important are water vapor, carbon dioxide, methane, and CFCs

Gross Domestic Product (GDP), n. An economic index that measures the monetary value of all goods bought and sold during a time period

homeostasis, n. The ability of an organism or system to maintain a constant temperature even while its surrounding environment changes

illth, n. A word coined by British economist John Ruskin to describe the negative effects of commercial activity; the opposite of *wealth*

inheritance, n. A gift received by children from their parents upon their parents' death; a gift received by all of us from previous generations or from the common creation

liquidity, n. The ability of an asset to be sold for cash

market, n. A socially created system in which goods and services can be bought and sold

negative marginal return, n. In economics, a situation in which the added loss or harm brought about by an activity exceeds the added benefits

ozone, n. A molecule containing three atoms of oxygen. In the upper atmosphere, it protects the earth from ultraviolet radiation; in the lower atmosphere, it is a harmful pollutant

permit, n. In a cap-and-trade system, a right to emit waste into a commons

Plimsoll line, n. A line painted on the hull of a ship that must always remain above water; a load line

precautionary principle, n. In situations of uncertain risk, the notion that it is better to be safe than sorry

property income, n. Income from stocks, bonds, real estate, and other forms of property

public trust doctrine, n. A common law doctrine that says that the state holds certain resources in trust for its citizens

rent, n. Colloquially, money paid to landlords by tenants; in classical economics, money paid to owners of a natural resource, such as land, the supply of which is fixed; most broadly, money paid to owners of any asset because of scarcity or market power

res communes, n. Things owned in common. In Roman law, this included rivers and shorelines, the air and wildlife

return on investment, n. In business, an investor's annual payback expressed as a percentage of the amount invested

royalty, n. A payment made to owners of a patent, copyright, or mineral right

scarce, adj. Colloquially, in short supply; the opposite of abundant. In economics, a thing is *scarce* if the demand for it exceeds the supply

scarcity rent, n. In economics, the amount paid by a buyer just because a thing is scarce; for example, the amount paid to a ticket scalper that exceeds the original price of the ticket

sink, n. A place, such as a landfill, into which wastes flow or are dumped

source, n. A place, such as a forest, from which resources are extracted

spectrum, n. The usable frequency range of radio waves

stratosphere, n. The layer of the atmosphere extending from about 6 to 15 miles above the earth's surface; includes the ozone layer

supply, n. In economics, the quantity of a good that is available in the market at a given price

sustainable, adj. Capable of continuing indefinitely; in economics, capable of providing for the living generation without diminishing the resources available to future generations

system, n. An ensemble of parts that work together to sustain a greater whole

systemic, adj. Applying to an entire system, not just to a part

tragedy of the commons, n. The destruction that can occur when there are no limits on use of a commons

troposphere, n. The layer of the atmosphere closest to the earth's surface; home to most of our air and weather

trust, n. A legal entity designed to hold and manage assets on behalf of beneficiaries

trustee, n. A person appointed to oversee the management of a trust

Who Owns the Sky?

Introduction

The Wealth Around Us

Oh beautiful for spacious skies,
For amber waves of grain,
For purple mountains' majesties
Above the fruited plain!

America, America,
God shed Thy grace on thee!
And crown Thy good with brotherhood,
From sea to shining sea!
—Katherine Lee Bates

1923
Ten million cars on U.S. roads; Coolidge declares
"the business of America is business"
Average conconcentration of carbon dioxide in the air:
304 *parts per million*
Average temperature at surface of the earth: 56.9°F

This book is about your inheritance, my inheritance, and our children's inheritance. I'm not talking about the money our parents may or may not have given us. If you were lucky enough to have been

1

born to rich parents, then you started life with a big advantage. That's your *individual* inheritance, and if you got one you should be grateful for it, because in truth, you did nothing to earn it.

The inheritance I'm talking about is much larger and, at the same time, less obvious. It's our inheritance of gifts we don't normally think we own. Things like air, water, and forests. These gifts are very valuable, perhaps even priceless. They're valuable for basic biological reasons—we can't live without them—and they're also valuable in an economic sense.

For every drop of gasoline we burn, we also burn oxygen and rely on the atmosphere to remove the wastes. Thus, no air, no cars (at least as we know them). When we watch *Who Wants to Be a Millionaire* or talk on our cell phones, we're using another gift of nature, the broadcast spectrum. No spectrum, no TV, and no Nokias. In other words, without the often invisible services of nature, our modern economy couldn't function and our standard of living would be much lower.

How much is our shared inheritance worth? While it's impossible to come up with an exact price tag, it's safe to say it's worth *trillions* of dollars. And even though we're physically destroying much of this wealth, its economic value—which derives in large part from its scarcity—is actually *rising*. Think about it: The more we pollute our free-flowing water, the more we pay for bottled clean water.

Well, you may ask, what good does this wealth do us if we never see it in cash? One answer is, this wealth is the basis for all we hold dear, including life itself. Even if we never see a penny in cash, we must preserve and protect it for creatures yet unborn.

But that's not my point in this book. My point, without belittling the previous one, is that we *can* and *should* turn some of our shared inheritance into cash. This can be done by (1) charging market prices for using our inherited assets, and (2) paying dividends to ourselves as their rightful inheritors. We should do this not out of greed, but out of concern for protecting these assets and passing them on, undiminished, to future generations.

Let's examine this proposition more closely. One reason we don't see our natural inheritance in cash is that *no one pays anything to use it.* Polluters use our air and water for free. Broadcasters use our airwaves for free. If Waste Management Inc. owned the sky, it would charge users whatever the market would bear. But we're not so businesslike. We give our assets away without charging a dime. This not only means we receive no cash. It also means we let our assets get abused.

If, in order to preserve our common assets, we need to charge for using them, two questions quickly arise: How will we set the prices? And to whom will the money go? These are deep economic and philosophic questions, yet they need to be answered, and answered soon.

The answers I offer in this book are simple: *markets* should set prices for our commonly inherited assets, and we should pay *ourselves.* I offer these answers as a successful business person who appreciates what markets and property rights can do. The key is to realize there's *wealth right in front of our noses,* if we would but see it and claim it. This book shows how we can do that.

Stormy Weather

In June 2000, while many parts of the United States experienced their highest recorded temperatures ever, a committee of experts working for the U.S. government issued a peer-reviewed assessment of the probable impacts of climate change. If nothing is done to reduce greenhouse gas emissions, the scientists said, average temperatures in the United States will rise 5 degrees to 10 degrees Farenheit over the next century. This warming will produce more frequent—and more intense—storms, droughts, heat waves, floods, and fires than we currently endure. Forests will undergo dramatic changes, including loss of sugar maples in the Northeast. In the West, a smaller snowpack will mean less water for dams to store, exacerbating current water shortages. In the Southeast, rising seas will devour beaches and wetlands, and coastal communities will be at even greater risk of violent storms.

The report was just one of perhaps hundreds that scientists have issued in the past decade. Though the numbers and details vary, the basic message doesn't: Unless we curb our emissions of greenhouse gases (most notably, carbon dioxide), we'll alter the basic conditions that have sustained life on Earth for three billion years.

The trouble is, carbon dioxide is an inescapable by-product of fossil fuel combustion, and the burning of oil, coal, and natural gas is what powers our industrial economy. Hence, the scientific reports have generated a fair amount of hand-wringing, but not a lot of action. Few Americans want to abandon the benefits cheap energy brings. So, for the moment, we're frozen in denial. We hear the knocking on the door; but no, we insist, it's not the Big Bad Wolf.

Nevertheless, our denial can't last forever. If human activity (and especially American activity) has altered our climate, we (both as a species and as a nation) will have crossed a historic divide. We will no longer be innocent, inconsequential beings. We will, collectively, have become a bull in a very precious china shop—that tiny nook in creation's handiwork that nourishes the only known life in the cosmos. And we will, collectively, have to change our carbon-burning habits.

Thus, at some point, we'll need to think about *how* we change—*how* we constrain our appetite for carbon-burning while we preserve, to the maximum extent possible, the freedoms and comforts we now enjoy. That *how* is this book's subject. This is thus a "how-to" book for citizens, politicians, and all who care about our long-term future.

The structure of the book is as follows. In the first five chapters, I explain why the earth's atmosphere is invaluable to us just as it is, and how we've nevertheless altered it dangerously. The reason for our high-risk behavior, I argue, is that markets don't recognize the sky's true scarcity. I propose to fix this market flaw with a nongovernmental institution—a U.S. Sky Trust—that charges market prices for polluting the atmosphere and pays each of us an equal dividend.

In the last three chapters, I expand my inquiry to other assets we've inherited together. Can they, like the sky, be protected through market mechanisms that reflect both the scarcity of the asset and our shared ownership? Can a new "common sector" be created through which the enormous wealth around us is both preserved and equitably shared? In this part of the book, I challenge conventional economic thinking and ask a lot of "what ifs." I emerge with a vision of the future that's brighter than you might expect.

Chapter 1

Winds of Change

Not I, not I, but the wind that blows through me . . .
—D. H. Lawrence

> *1942*
> *World War II rages; author is born*
> *Carbon dioxide concentration in the air: 298 parts per million*
> *Average temperature at surface of the earth: 57.4°F*

M y parents weren't rich. Children of immigrants, they came of age in the Great Depression with literally nothing. They worked hard, saved a lot, and profited from the broad rise of stocks that characterized the fifties and sixties. They paid for my education at Harvard. When I turned thirty, they gave me enough for a down payment on a home in San Francisco I still own. When I started a business at age thirty-four, they lent me capital and then forgave the loan. When my father died two decades later, he left me more. I in turn will leave my two sons more than my parents left me. That's my family economic history in a nutshell. I've been lucky, and I'm profoundly grateful for my good fortune.

At the same time, I'm acutely aware that my good fortune isn't shared by all. Most children are born with little or no individual inheritance. They may receive their parents' love and tutelage—gifts of inestimable value—but they don't get the chits for a superior education, a down payment on a home, or a business start-up.

Why don't they? Bad luck, you might say, since no child deserves an inheritance any more than any other. But when, in the lottery of life, bad luck so persistently outweighs good, you must conclude that the lottery itself is flawed.

That is, in fact, a realization I came to early in life. It's hard for me to pinpoint the precise moment this realization hit me—certainly, my parents' modest means during my early years, their kitchen-table talk of the Depression, and their repeated invocations of hard work and thrift all contributed. So did riding the subways of New York City and looking at the forlorn faces of my fellow passengers.

After college, my first jobs were as a journalist. I worked in Lowell, Massachusetts, on the local newspaper, *The Sun,* then for *Newsweek* in Washington and *The New Republic* in San Francisco. I covered politics inside the Beltway and social movements outside it.

The epiphany wasn't that I could get rich—my interest then, as it still is today, was in making the world a little fairer. My epiphany was that the market is mightier than the pen, and consequently, that the way to make the world fairer was to go into business. And so, in 1976, I cofounded a solar energy company with five friends. The idea was, we'd design and install solar heating systems, thereby reducing the use of fossil fuels and nuclear power. This would be good for nature. At the same time, we'd run the business as a worker-owned cooperative. This would be good for the workers, and maybe even for the bottom line.

We discovered a niche that made sense in urban San Francisco: central solar water heating systems for apartment buildings. We invented ingenious ways to finance these systems so their owners enjoyed immediate positive cash flow. We learned how to bid, design, and manage commercial-scale projects costing hundreds of thousands of dollars, how to use cranes and computers, and how to take advantage of tax preferences.

Our annual sales rose to $2 million, and we had thirty-five employee-owners at our peak.

Though the business succeeded, I was bothered by the fact that what really sold our product was tax credits. I wanted to compete with other energy sources on a flat playing field. And I worried that what government had given, government could also take away.

As I pondered this, I realized other energy providers also got subsidies. Thanks to numerous loopholes, oil companies paid little in the way of federal income taxes. Nuclear companies benefited from decades of government research, going all the way back to the Manhattan Project. Moreover, these competitors sold energy at prices that didn't include all costs. Coal-burning power plants paid nothing for the air they polluted and much too little for the land they destroyed by strip-mining. Oil companies paid nothing for the airplanes, ships, and soldiers that defended the Persian Gulf. Nuclear power sellers benefited from subsidized disaster insurance and a blank check on future costs of waste disposal. In short, I realized that what's included in, or excluded from, every business's cost of goods sold is often arbitrary and political.

Then Ronald Reagan was elected, solar tax credits were abolished, and across America solar companies—including ours—shut their doors.

The next business I co-founded, Working Assets, began as a socially screened money fund. As vice president in charge of marketing, I wrote and designed our first full-page ad. Against an ominous image of a nuclear cooling tower, my headline proclaimed: "It's 11 p.m. Do you know where your money is?" The copy said that if your money was in an ordinary bank, it was probably building nuclear power plants, buying bombs, or financing apartheid in South Africa. If, however, you moved your money to Working Assets, we'd invest it in things like renewable energy, family farming, and higher education. What was more, we'd pay you a competitive rate of interest, so you wouldn't sacrifice anything to do good.

People read the ad and mailed us checks. Soon we'd received over $100 million and were listed in the *Wall Street Journal*. It astounded me that people trusted perfect strangers with large chunks of their savings—after all, the folks who mailed us money didn't know us from Adam. Later, I realized it wasn't *us* they trusted, but the American financial system. That trusted system is thus a valuable societal asset—but more about such assets later.

A few cynics at the time contended that social screening of investments was just a marketing gimmick that would do little, if anything, to build a better world. There's so much capital moving about, they argued, that no company *needed* Working Assets' dollars; therefore our leverage was essentially nil. While this was technically true, I saw our influence as being subtler than that, yet nonetheless real. Yes, giant corporations would barely quiver in our financial shadow, but over time, they'd take note. We and our customers would help define higher standards of corporate behavior. We'd honor the better companies not just with capital, but with praise. Conversely, we'd damn the laggards by withholding not only money but respect. Others would emulate us, and public awareness would grow. Eventually, society would expect more from corporations, and corporations would compete to meet those higher expectations. They'd feel *market pressure* not to support oppressive regimes, ignore environmental rules, or pay appalling wages. The gains that ultimately ensued would be real and tangible.

We coined a word: *greentapping*. It meant *diverting money within the market to good uses*. I became intrigued with the idea. Shifting money within markets seemed a useful way to make the world fairer. I contemplated other ways to do this.

One day I realized people *spend* a lot more than they *save*. Inspired by this insight, I invented a new product that was a guilty spender's dream—the Working Assets Visa Card, or *Plastic With Purpose*. Every time a cardholder made a purchase using a Working Assets Visa Card, we donated to nonprofit groups working for peace, human rights, economic justice, and a cleaner environment, at no cost to the cardholder. The donation came from the service charge paid by the merchant. Our hope was that thousands of Americans would use the card, and over time shift millions of dollars to worthy causes.

Again to my amazement, what we hoped for soon happened. And we extended the concept to long-distance telephone service. We made a deal with Sprint to re-sell extra capacity on their fiber-optic network. Every time a customer called, we donated 1 percent of their charges to the same nonprofit groups supported by our credit card, at no cost to the caller. Since our long-distance rates were competitive with other carriers, there was nothing for our customers to lose.

By this time I was president of the company and my entrepreneurial audacity was soaring. I decided a phone company could do more than shift money; it could also strengthen democracy.

How so? A phone company, it turns out, has two assets that can spur democratic dialogue. First, it mails bills to its customers every month. The typical phone bill is just a list of calls and charges. How boring and wasteful! Why not use the same envelope and paper, I reasoned, to carry timely political information? For example, if an important vote is coming up in Congress, why not let citizens know about it and help them express their opinions? This is what we did on page 1 of every phone bill.

The other thing a phone company has, of course, is phone lines. It's not a big expense to let customers call their Congress members, or the president, or corporate officials, and talk with them or their aides for a few minutes. So when we informed our customers of pending decisions, we also let them call the relevant decision makers at no charge. We considered this a modest contribution to free speech.

Our phone service was an even bigger hit than our earlier products. By 2001 we'd donated more than $25 million to scores of worthy nonprofits, and generated over a million phone calls to government and corporate decision makers. In short, we were using the market to achieve social goals, and on the side, we were making a profit.

Market Mechanisms

After twenty years as a capitalist, I decided to hang up my cleats. I'd learned an immense amount. I'd found that while markets can be cruelly limiting, they can also be exciting and liberating. If you pay your bills, you can pretty much do what you want. You can be fair to your workers and generous to your community. You can even use markets to protect the environment or make society more democratic, if that's your inclination.

Nevertheless, there are limits to what a single business can do. When I was president of Working Assets, I used to give a speech to incoming employees. Our mission, I'd say, is to change the genetic code of corporations. "The dominant DNA," I explained, "is to make profits first and foremost. Our genes are different. We take money off our *top* line and give it back to the world which makes our existence possible. Giving back to the world isn't something we think about *after* we make a profit—it's part of our cost of doing business. It's a cost we pay up front. Our mission is to out-compete companies who don't pay this cost, and thereby not only survive, but eventually change corporate DNA."

In the years since leaving Working Assets, I've had time to ponder that vision a bit more. It was, without doubt, part of the reason many employees and customers came to Working Assets. But as a strategy for changing the world, it was weak. Waiting for "fitter" genes to triumph could take generations—and I don't think the earth can wait that long. Moreover, I'm not sure Working Assets' genes are in fact "fitter," as fitness is defined in today's markets. Firms that voluntarily pay added costs rarely gain a competitive advantage; if anything, the reverse is probably true.

My pondering accelerated when I entered the world of American think tanks. My first senior fellowship was at Redefining Progress, a stew of mostly young intellectuals whose chosen mission was to make capitalism more sustainable and equitable *through market mechanisms.* RP, as it was called, had an attitude. Big problems, the group said, need big solutions. In fact, they need *systemic* solutions. We shouldn't use Band-Aids when the organism is dying of cancer. We should cure the disease rather than paper over the symptoms.

I liked this cheekiness, but it posed an obvious question. Could systemic solutions be market-based? Or did they, by their very nature, require persistent government intervention? RP's answer was that systemic change may require government intervention to *create* market mechanisms, but once the mechanisms are up and running, markets can take over. Government's role is to set boundaries, define property rights, and collect taxes (up to a point), and to use those tools to shape markets.

Then, the combination of those tools with the natural dynamism of markets can create systemic change.

As a business person I felt comfortable with this approach. My role was to push the scholars to put real meat on the table. The meat they came up with, however, struck me as ineffective and improbable. Their favored approach was "tax shifting." By taxing "bads" instead of "goods," RP argued, government could tilt markets toward sustainability and fairness. All that's needed is enough wise and courageous politicians.

My skepticism about in tax tinkering derived from experience and memory. I remembered the transience of solar tax credits in the 1970s. I remembered when high incomes were taxed at 70 percent and the U.S. Treasury was expected to rectify the uneven outcomes of the market. I remembered when "fine-tuning" of federal taxing and spending was supposed to tranquilize the business cycle. In short, I remembered enough to doubt that lasting systemic change could be teased out of the ebb and flow of tax politics. My preferred tools for lasting systemic change were boundaries (for sustainability) and property rights (for equity).

Fortuitously, another San Francisco think tank, the Corporation for Enterprise Development, was of like mind. The founder of CFED, Robert Friedman, was a strong believer in property ownership by the poor; he saw such ownership as a key to breaking the intergenerational transmission of poverty. He invited me to explore how an expansion of property rights that benefited the poor could simultaneously protect nature.

There were two questions I contemplated at CFED. First, how can we make markets respect the boundaries nature is signaling us not to cross? In particular, how can we make markets recognize there's only so much carbon dioxide the sky can safely absorb? Second, how can more Americans—in fact, *every* American—have the good luck of birth that I had: a little inherited capital to help with education, first home purchase, or starting a business (if not all three)?

I imagined the answers to these two questions might intersect, but I wasn't sure how. Soon, however, a line of thinking emerged. If we limit emissions into the sky, markets will see the sky as scarce. If markets see the sky as scarce, it will no longer be free. If polluters must pay to use the sky, the sky will become a hugely valuable asset. If the sky is a hugely valuable asset, who should own it? Is there a way *all* of us can own it—a way all of us can benefit from this valuable shared inheritance?

The trick, it seemed to me, was to create a financial institution—perhaps similar to a mutual fund—to own and manage the sky on behalf of millions of owners. Maybe, I mused, there's a business opportunity here. I soon concluded, however, that the sky can't be managed for profit. The sky is a sacred trust, a shared inheritance we must pass on intact to our heirs. Hence the proper entity to own it is a trust.

Chapter 2

The Sky Is Filling!

This most excellent canopy, the air, look you, this brave
o'er-hanging firmament, this majestical roof fretted with
golden fire, why, it appears no other thing to me but a
foul and pestilent congregation of vapours.

—*Hamlet* (Act 2, Scene 2)

1952
Suburbia spreads; Eisenhower is elected.
Carbon dioxide concentration in the air: 312 parts per million
Average temperature at surface of the earth: 57.3°F

If you happen to be reading this book on an airplane (my favorite
place to read), you're in an ideal spot. Look out the window for
a moment. Ignore all efforts by the airline (food, movies, maga-
zines) to distract you from doing this. Notice that you're floating in
a metal tube, about seven miles above the earth's surface. Notice
that your cabin is pressurized. Realize that the air immediately outside your window is thick enough to keep your tube from falling,
but not thick enough for you to breathe. Realize that the white
wisps of water vapor you see are cleansing the earth's limited supply

of freshwater. Realize that you're just a few score miles from the void of outer space.

If you're not in an airplane, walk outside. Lie with your back on the ground and your eyes looking up. Gaze at the sky for about ten minutes. Ignore all efforts of other humans to distract you from doing this. Listen to the sounds of birds, wind, traffic. Inhale through your nose, then exhale deeply. Feel the taste and texture of the air, its moisture, its tingle. Notice that you don't normally look at the sky this way; your head and neck swivel horizontally, not vertically. Notice that you can't look directly at the sun; it's just too intense. If it's nighttime, notice those other suns billions of light-years away; do you wonder how they got there? Notice that the air is constantly moving. Realize that the gas flowing in and out of your lungs is the same gas that touches every creature that ever lived or will live (minus a few whose niches are deep under water). Realize that, through the air, you're physically connected to pretty much the entire biosphere.

Heaven and Earthlings

There's nothing more fundamental to us than the sky—our sky, our *unique* sky. We're sky animals. We live on land but *in* sky. We inhale from and exhale into it about fifteen thousand times a day. We fly in airplanes and communicate with cell phones. We are to air as fish are to water.

The atmosphere is the most important part of the biosphere for humans and all life. Yet nowadays, despite our physical dependence on the sky, we're mentally cut off from it. We spend most of our lives indoors, and when we move about, it's usually inside a bubble we've built. Most of the time, the air we breathe is processed in some mechanical way. In many of our workplaces, it's not even possible to open windows. At night our artificial torches are so bright we can barely see the stars. So most of us pay little attention to the sky.

Our ancestors connected much more intimately with the sky than we do. Without tall buildings and electric lights, they saw the sky day and night. And they not only saw it, they *studied* it. They came to know the clouds and winds, the clues to the sky's moods, because their crops and daily routines depended on those moods. The sun was their clock. If they sailed, they used wind for power and stars as guides.

The sky wasn't only their daily companion, it was home to their gods. In Greek, Hebrew, and the Germanic and Romance languages (English excepted), the same word denotes "sky" and "heaven." In the ancient imagination, divine personalities roamed the sky, tossing thunderbolts, slaying enemies, making love, tinkering in human affairs. Later ancestors came to believe that humans who lived righteously would ascend to the sky. Music was a form of celestial harmony. In short, the sky was a holy and magical place.

The Scientific Revolution changed all that. In the new, mechanistic view of the world, the sky was devoid of animation or divinity. It was a sea of gases, period. Only in the latter part of the twentieth century did scientists begin to see how intimately sky and life are connected.

What the Sky Does for Us

The first thing to remember about the sky is how thin it is. Though we can't see its outer edge from our vantage point on the earth's surface, that outer edge is not far away. In fact, if we could walk vertically at the same speed we walk horizontally, we'd reach it in just a few hours. To put it another way, if the earth were an apple, the atmosphere would be about as thick as its peel.

The second thing to remember about the sky is that it isn't uniform. Modern scientists have identified five distinct layers. The bottom layer, closest to the earth's surface, contains most of the air—a mix of nitrogen, oxygen, and a few trace gases. This layer, known as the troposphere, is agitated by hot and cold winds, pressure fronts, and moisture. It gives us our weather and climate.

Starting about six miles up—roughly the altitude of Mt. Everest—is a sparse, stable region known as the stratosphere, where jet planes like to cruise. The stratosphere is home to an unusual form of oxygen called ozone. Next come the mesosphere, the ionosphere, and the thermosphere, each increasingly empty, until finally, about two hundred miles up, comes the black void of space.

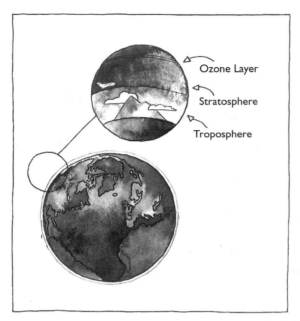

Figure 1. The Earth's Atmosphere

The third and most important thing to remember about the sky is that there's a lot going on up there that benefits humans and other species. Here's a short list of what the sky, at various altitudes, does for us:

- It shields us from asteroids and meteors. (See all those craters on the moon? You don't see them on Earth.)

- It protects us from harmful ultraviolet rays. (Ultraviolet rays burn the skin, cause skin cancer and cataracts, and damage vegetation. Thank those ozone molecules for blocking them.)

- It maintains the earth's temperature within a range suitable to life. (You wouldn't want to winter on Venus. Its surface is far hotter that it would otherwise be because its atmosphere is 96 percent carbon dioxide.)

- It continuously replenishes our supply of freshwater. (Less than 1 percent of the water on Earth is unsalted. We'd have run out of it long ago if the sky didn't replenish it.)

- It delivers oxygen to our lungs and machines. (Yes, our cars as well as our bodies burn oxygen.)
- It cycles and recycles nearly all the elements and nutrients used by living organisms.
- It absorbs our exhausts and moves them somewhere else. (What a wonderful convenience to have the sky just whisk this stuff away!)
- It bounces radio signals back to Earth. (This was handy before we had satellites.)
- It blows large boats across the oceans and powers windmills.
- It lifts 400-ton jetliners above the highest mountains and lets them zip around the world at breakneck speeds.
- It carries sound and lets us talk to each other.

The sky has graciously performed these services for millions of years, without once presenting a bill. Unfortunately, the sky's ability to keep doing these wonderful things for us isn't assured. Many of its services require a precise mix of gases in the air, and that mix is threatened by human activities.

Consider temperature. Like the human body, the earth and its biosphere are *homeostatic*—that is, they maintain steady temperatures, regardless of what's going on around them. (Bear in mind that the sun's heat has risen 25 percent since the earth was formed; it's the kind of star that gets hotter as it gets older.) The atmosphere is critical to the earth's temperature stability, which in turn is critical to life. The key is the precise concentration of trace gases in the air. The major atmospheric gases—nitrogen and oxygen, which make up 98 percent of the air—play almost no role in determining temperature. But water vapor, carbon dioxide, and methane, which together make up less than 1 percent of the atmosphere, keep the earth's temperature within life's narrow comfort zone.

These are the so-called greenhouse gases. Like the panes of a greenhouse, they let heat from the sun pass through, but trap heat that radiates back. If the concentration of greenhouse gases thins, more heat escapes and the earth cools. Conversely, if the concentration of greenhouse gases thickens, more heat is trapped and the earth gets warmer. Just as when we add or remove a bed blanket, a small change in the thickness of our atmospheric blanket makes us feel very different.

Or consider ultraviolet protection. Fortunately for life on Earth, it doesn't take a lot of molecules to block ultraviolet rays: Consider what a fine job is done by a thin film of sunblock on your skin. Like Coppertone, the ozone layer in the stratosphere is effective but thin. This thinness implies fragility; a small loss of ozone will let harmful rays through.

Or consider how lucky we are that oxygen makes up 21 percent of our air at sea level. If there were less oxygen in the air, we couldn't breathe. If there were more, everything would catch fire.

In short, our unique sky is a miraculous gift. It's "just right" as it is, and it's able to *stay* just right without our help. This self-regulating stability is precious.

What We Do to the Sky

For most of our million-year residence on Earth, humans left the sky alone. Like other animals, we inhaled oxygen (our cellular fuel) and exhaled carbon dioxide (a residue of cellular energy production). We also cut a few trees and built a few fires. But that was pretty much it.

It's only lately, in the past two hundred years, that our use of the sky has changed fundamentally. The change began with James Watt's steam engine, accelerated after Thomas Edison's electric inventions, and exploded after Karl Benz's internal combustion engine. Suddenly, the atmosphere became more than an extension of our lungs. It became a dump for our machines, factories, and furnaces.

At first, this increase in sky use went unnoticed. In cities like New York, the change people saw—and very much appreciated—was the disappearance of horse manure from the streets. No one realized that these animal droppings were being replaced by a far larger volume of automobile droppings. Svante Arrhenius, an eminent Swedish chemist, did warn in 1896 that carbon dioxide could in due time heat up the planet. But people paid little heed. Soon Henry Ford was making Model Ts and the world was falling in love with them. For Americans in particular, the car became the ultimate symbol of freedom, mobility, and status.

CFCs

Other inventions soon added to the outpouring of gases. Consider the ill-fated creations of Thomas Midgely Jr. Born in 1889, Midgely was an industrial chemist who, while working at General Motors, discovered that adding lead to gasoline stopped engine knocking and boosted the power of cars dramatically. "Ethyl," or leaded gas, was introduced, and the Ethyl Corporation, GM's new joint venture with Standard Oil of New Jersey, boomed.

After this triumph, Midgely was asked to find a safe refrigerant for GM's Frigidaire subsidiary (early refrigerants were toxic or flammable). In 1928 he created a class of compounds called chlorofluorocarbons, or CFCs. These new substances were described as "miracle chemicals." They're inert (and therefore don't catch fire), nontoxic, and noncorrosive—and they're superb as refrigerants, industrial solvents, and aerosols. Billions of tons have since been produced by DuPont (which partially owned GM) and many other companies around the world.

Midgely fell into poor health and committed suicide in 1944, a few decades before the full impact of his inventions became known. We now know that lead in gasoline causes mental and bodily deterioration in humans, while chlorine in CFCs floats to the stratosphere and breaks down the ozone molecules that block ultraviolet rays. This latter discovery—made in 1974 by two chemists at the University of California—was an extraordinary confirmation not only of the law of unforeseen consequences, but also of the fact that, in our universe, everything is connected to everything else.

By the 1950s, visible changes in the air began to appear. In many cities there was a brown haze in the sky that damaged people's lungs and eyes. The word "smog" was coined to describe this new haze, whose ingredients included by-products of gasoline combustion. In mountain-ringed cities like Los Angeles and Denver, the smog often got so noxious that people stayed indoors on bad air days.

Around the same time, forests and lakes in the Northeast began to die from acid rain. One cause of this lethal precipitation was the sulfur contained in coal burned by midwestern power plants. When this coal was burned, sulfur particles rose into the sky, traveled eastward with the winds, and mixed with water vapor to form sulfuric acid. When the acid came down, it killed trees and fish.

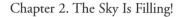

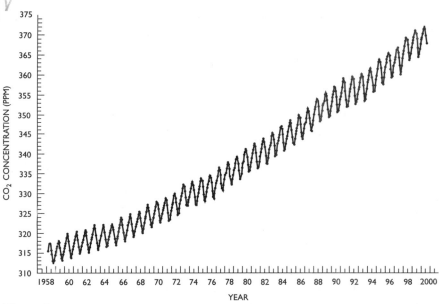

Figure 2. The Keeling Curve

Every year since 1958, Charles Keeling has measured the atmospheric concentrations of carbon dioxide on top of Mauna Loa in Hawaii. The unbroken trend is upward. The "squiggles" are due to seasonal variations (concentrations are lower in summer when plants consume more carbon dioxide).

Source: National Oceanic and Atmospheric Administration, Climate Monitoring and Diagnostics Laboratory.

Eventually scientists began to reconsider Arrhenius. A Harvard professor, Roger Revelle, prodded Charles Keeling, of the Scripps Institute for Oceanography, to sample carbon dioxide concentrations at the top of Mauna Loa in Hawaii. The resulting "Keeling curve" is now one of the most famous graphs in earth science. It shows the concentration of carbon dioxide rising steadily from 1958 on.

Later research, probing air bubbles deep in Antarctic ice, traced carbon dioxide concentrations backward for thousands of years. The results show a strong correlation between carbon dioxide and average global temperatures. They also show that before cars and power plants, the carbon dioxide concentration was 280 parts per million. Now it's 360 parts per million, and before long it will be double the pre-industrial level.

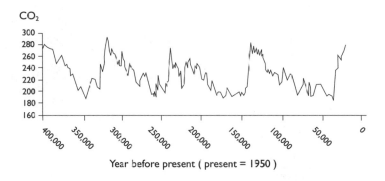

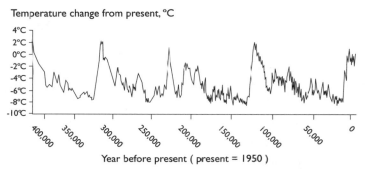

Figure 3. Temperature and Carbon Dioxide Concentrations over 160,000 Years
These data were computed by scientists who drilled a mile-deep hole in an Antarctic glacier. They extracted an ice cylinder representing water that fell as snow up to 160,000 years ago. From air bubbles in the ice they were able to estimate ancient temperatures and carbon dioxide concentrations.
Source: Center for the Study of Carbon Dioxide and Global Change <http://www. co2science.org>

Carbon Cravings

Carbon dioxide, the largest waste product of our economy, is a sneaky pollutant. It's invisible to our eyes and noses, and unlike its sister carbon monoxide, isn't directly toxic to humans. The danger from carbon dioxide lies solely, but still ominously, in its *overabundance.* As long as humans merely exhale, and don't burn trees or fossil fuels, carbon dioxide is no bother. As long as we burn trees and fossil fuels in moderation—say, at 1900 or even 1950 levels—carbon dioxide isn't a huge worry. But when we destroy half the earth's forests and saturate it with carbon-burning cars and power plants, *then* our greenhouse blanket thickens, and this is a serious threat.

The first consequences of our thickening greenhouse blanket are now visible to the naked eye. Ice shelves in Antarctica are melting. Coral reefs in the Indian Ocean are dying. Winters in North America are starting later. Pacific islands are sinking under rising seas. Floods, hurricanes, droughts, and blizzards are increasing in frequency and severity. Though none of these disasters can be blamed solely on thicker levels of carbon dioxide, the signals are ominous. More carbon dioxide in the atmosphere means more heat in the atmosphere; more heat in the atmosphere means more water that evaporates and more energy that dissipates as wind. Insurance companies, who count these things, say that twenty-one of the twenty-five worst natural disasters in history have occurred in the past decade, and sixteen of these involved wind and water.

By the 1990s, governments had officially recognized that Chicken Little had it *almost* right. The sky isn't falling, but it *is* filling. It can safely absorb only so much ozone-eating chlorine, acid-brewing sulfur, and heat-trapping carbon dioxide—and we're now reaching those limits. Putting it another way, it's not oil we're running out of, it's *sky*.

A few observers, it should be noted, saw the sky shortage coming. One early warning came from Kenneth Boulding, an American economist. "The shadow of the future is indeed falling over our spendthrift merriment," Boulding warned in 1966. "Oddly enough, it seems to be in pollution rather than in exhaustion that the problem is first becoming salient. Los Angeles has run out of air, Lake Erie has become a cesspool, the oceans are full of lead and DDT, and the atmosphere may become man's major problem in another generation, at the rate at which we are filling it up with gunk."

Indeed, a generation later, Boulding's premonition was echoed by a U.S. senator from Tennessee, Al Gore Jr. "The total volume of all the air in the world is actually quite small compared to the enormity of the earth," Gore wrote. "And we are filling it up, profoundly changing its makeup, every hour of every day, everywhere on the earth."

The End of Spacious Skies

When Katherine Lee Bates, a young poet, climbed Pikes Peak in 1893, what she saw in every direction was vastness: vast skies, vast mountains, vast plains. Inspired, she wrote the poem we sing today as "America the Beautiful." It's worth remembering as we sing her words that America *has* been blessed with a profusion of natural gifts. But vast as these gifts are, they're not infinite. In particular, the sky isn't as spacious as Bates imagined, nor is it a gift solely to America.

What does it mean to say we're running out of sky? Will the sky disappear one day, leaving an airless globe like the moon? Fortunately, nothing that extreme will happen. The shortage of sky is more subtle.

The shortage of sky is different from the shortage of oil. To paraphrase an old beer commercial, "When you're out of oil, you're out of oil." There simply isn't any more of it—or any more you can feasibly extract. The sky, by contrast, will always be there. But it will be a different sky with different gases in it. These gases will *fit;* there's no lack of space for them. But adding new gases to the mix will disrupt some of the nice things the sky now does for us, and *that* is the limiting factor.

It may be helpful here to say a bit about systems. Like an orchestra, a system is an ensemble of many parts, with a set of rules and feedback loops that, most of the time, help the parts work together smoothly. There are, however, two types of feedback loops: a virtuous kind and a perverse kind. In virtuous loops (which scientists, oddly enough, call "negative"), if one part of the system gets out of line, another part of the system will bring it back. In perverse loops (which scientists call "positive"), one bad event triggers another, and the whole system can spiral into disequilibrium.

The human economy is a large system containing many smaller systems. So is nature. In the natural as well as the human world, there are stresses and strains on every system. In a good system—a *long-lasting* system—the virtuous feedback loops respond effectively to these stresses. Big problems can arise, however, if perverse feedback is triggered. This would occur, for example, if the thermostat on your wall suddenly turned your heater *on* as the room got hotter, instead of turning it *off.* Because of the malfunctioning thermostat, the room would get hotter and hotter, rather than stay at the desired temperature. If other parts of the system were designed to work at, or near, the desired temperature, they too would soon cease to work.

All of which makes the question "What kind of stress can a system tolerate?" a critical one. A strain that can be offset by virtuous feedback is no big deal. A strain that triggers perverse feedback, on the other hand, can be disastrous. Sometimes there's a tipping point after which a little strain cascades into catastrophe. What's the straw that will break the camel's back? What's the stress that the system won't tolerate? Most of the time we simply don't know. There are no flashing lights that say, "Proceed this far, but no farther." Thus the uncertainty that surrounds all complex systems.

Scientists deal with this uncertainty by establishing thresholds—best guesses, really, as to how much stress a system can tolerate. For example, we know the human body can tolerate large amounts of some chemicals, and very small amounts of others. Oreo cookies can be consumed in quantity; arsenic cannot. Alcohol is somewhere in the middle. Similarly, a small amount of plutonium will wreak havoc in the biosphere. Carbon dioxide, on the other hand, is harmless in small doses (that's why Coke puts it in soft drinks), but causes global overheating when introduced in large quantities.

It may also be useful to say a bit about sinks. The term *sink*, as used by scientists and economists, means a place that's capable of absorbing wastes. Its opposite is a *source*, a place from which things come. The human economy, in its broadest sense, can be said to work like this: We take raw materials from sources, process them with labor and capital, and dump the wastes into sinks. As we'll see later, this is an oversimplified picture that assumes sources and sinks are infinite. But it's the way most economists view things today.

Sinks come in many shapes and sizes. A landfill outside your town is a sink. So is the river running through town, the air above town, and the ground in and around town. Maybe there's a water table underneath you—that, too, is a sink. Your lungs, body fat, liver, and kidneys—they, too, are sinks of a sort.

In the past, when people talked about running out of things, what they typically had in mind were sources. Thomas Malthus, back in the early nineteenth century, was afraid we'd run out of land and water to grow food. In 1968, the controversial *Limits to Growth* predicted we'd run out of oil, water, and lots of other stuff.

The authors of these books were deemed "doomsayers." They were challenged by optimists who said that human ingenuity would more than compensate for physical shortages. Prominent among the optimists was the late economist Julian Simon, who made a famous bet with one of the leading pessimists, ecologist Paul Ehrlich.

In 1980, Simon bet Ehrlich $1,000 that in ten years the prices of any raw materials Erhlich named would fall rather than rise. If this happened, Simon argued, it would prove we weren't running out of the materials. Ehrlich chose minerals like crude oil, copper, chrome, nickel, tin, and tungsten. A decade later, all their prices had fallen (in constant dollars), and Erhlich paid up.

What's striking about this bet is that Ehrlich *could have won* if he'd focused on sinks. During the 1980s, pollution soared. Air, water, and soils were pumped full of chemicals that didn't belong there. If nature's waste-absorbing capacities had been commodities like copper, tungsten, and oil, their prices would surely have risen.

Ehrlich, of course, was no fool. Perhaps the reason he *didn't* bet on sinks was that Simon wouldn't let him. Simon, being an economist, would have insisted that *prices* be the ultimate judge of scarcity—and in the 1980s, a time when almost everything had a price, sinks didn't. The absorbing capacities of nature were *not* commodities like copper, tungsten, and oil. There were no markets for them, and hence no prices.

Today, the situation is clear: It's sinks, not sources, we're running out of. Metals are plentiful, and silicon—the prime ingredient of the information economy—is the most abundant mineral on Earth. There are even plenty of fossil fuels in the ground—enough coal, it's been calculated, for another half millennium.

The problem is, where do we put our voluminous wastes? Molecules never disappear; they always go *somewhere,* and gravity keeps them tied to the earth. So the ability of the biosphere to absorb them must always be taken into account. How do we store radioactive wastes for ten thousand years when no government has ever lasted more than a thousand? Where do we stash the fumes of fossil fuels after we burn them? What happens to long-lasting chemicals that mimic human hormones, or destroy stratospheric ozone, after they've been dispersed in the air?

Sometimes I think of the sky as a big kitchen sink. If the sink drains as fast as it fills, everything's okay, but if it fills faster than it drains, we're in trouble. The bigger the difference between inflow and outflow, the more trouble we're in. Scientists estimate it takes about a hundred years for a carbon dioxide molecule to leave the sky. Since the stuff's pouring in much faster than that, we're in big trouble indeed.

That, in a nutshell, is the sink problem. Fortunately, it's solvable. And the solution begins with drawing a line.

The Gift of Samuel Plimsoll

There are two dilemmas regarding thresholds in systems. One, as noted earlier, is the difficulty of knowing exactly where the thresholds are. The other is, given the uncertainties involved, how much of a safety margin should we allow? Do we go right to the edge of danger, or do we leave a little wiggle room?

In scientific and policy parlance, the idea of leaving wiggle room is known as the *precautionary principle.* Since nature is full of surprises, the precautionary principle says we ought to err on the side of caution. The preference for caution is especially relevant when the potential consequences are grave and irreversible. In practice, this means decision makers should act in advance of scientific certainty to prevent potentially serious harm to humans and the environment. Our attitude today, however, is very much the opposite: dump first and deal with consequences later. The faster we dump, of course, the sooner we approach the threshold. That's why it's useful to draw a line—almost *any* line—to leave room for future maneuvering.

The idea of a "load line" was invented in 1870 by Samuel Plimsoll, a member of England's Parliament. In Plimsoll's times, British merchant ships roamed the world. But sailing was a hazardous business.

There were no undersea telegraph cables or shipboard radios to signal the fate of a ship and her crew. Once their masts sank below the horizon, ships could disappear for months. The last word was often a posting at Lloyd's: Missing, presumed lost. Part of the danger derived from the shipowners' desire to maximize profits. They'd load up with so much cargo that ships became unseaworthy. And as ships sank, sailors died.

Plimsoll exposed many bad practices by shipowners. Eventually, he won legislation requiring that a load line be painted on the hull of every large vessel. If the load line was underwater, the ship couldn't leave harbor. The location of the line was calculated from many factors: the structural strength of the ship, the height of the deck, the shape of the hull, and so forth. The days of "coffin ships" soon ended.

Now, 130 years later, it's time to draw another kind of Plimsoll line, this time in the sky. In this case the line won't say "This boat is full, no cargo beyond this point." It will say "This sky is full, no carbon dioxide beyond this point."

Where do we draw this line? The answer isn't known with certainty. Many factors are involved, including how much of a safety buffer we want. But since the Rio Treaty of 1992, in which the world agreed that human-caused climate change must be stopped, scientists have been working on this question. In 1995, the Intergovernmental Panel on Climate Change—a consortium of twenty-five hundred scientists worldwide—issued its consensus conclusion: The world must reduce total carbon emissions by 60 percent.

Let me repeat that statement, because it's important: *The world must reduce total carbon emissions by 60 percent.* That's 60 percent below the *1990* total. As this is written in 2001, we're emitting 15 percent *more* than we did in 1990. What's more, the scientists' recommended cut is *global.* Since the United States is the world's largest carbon emitter, we'll have to cut *more* than other countries if the global sky is to be equitably shared. The bottom line is that the United States must prepare to cut its carbon emissions by *90 percent* during the next half century (that is, 90 percent below our current level). And this is no mean task.

That number, of course, comes from scientists; it has yet to be officially accepted by our government. But there it is: the handwriting on the wall, the Plimsoll line in the air. It may be high or it may be low. But we probably shouldn't treat human survival as if it were a roll of the dice in Las Vegas. We probably should take this Plimsoll line seriously.

Scarcity Is Wealth

Okay. So sinks are scarce and the sky's running out and we're dangerously close to an edge. What does this have to do with wealth?

Here's a dirty little secret: Scarcity *is* wealth. I know this sounds counterintuitive. Intuitively, abundance is wealth and scarcity is poverty. But in the wondrous world of markets, that's not how it works.

Adam Smith, the father of modern economics, was right on the money when he said, "The word 'value' has two different meanings . . . The one may be called 'value in use'; the other, 'value in exchange.' The things which have the greatest value in use have frequently little or no value in exchange; and, on the contrary, those which have the greatest value in exchange have frequently little or no value in use. Nothing is more useful than water: but it will purchase scarce anything. A diamond, on the contrary, has scarce value in use; but a great quantity of other goods may frequently be had in exchange for it."

Smith, of course, lived long before a bottle of Perrier cost more than a liter of oil. But his "water and diamonds" paradox has become a standard teaching in economics. What something sells for in a market—its exchange value—depends on the interplay between supply and demand. The scarcer the supply, the higher the price. Water is plentiful and therefore cheap; that water is essential to life, and diamonds inconsequential, makes no difference. Diamonds are rare and therefore expensive. The only things markets truly care about are supply and demand.

This can be stated another way. In markets, less is often more. The scarcer the supply of a commodity, the more you can sell it for. Economists have a name for this less-is-more phenomenon: They call it *scarcity*

Adam Smith

rent. Scarcity rent is what owners of highly demanded things collect from other people *just because of scarcity.* The *Mona Lisa,* for example, has a high scarcity rent because there's big demand for it and only one original. In general, the scarcer (relative to demand) things such as buildable land, Mark McGwire home run balls, and New York taxi medallions are, the higher their scarcity rents.

Scarcity rent is not to be confused with the rent you pay your landlord. Only part of what you pay your landlord—the part that reflects the value of land in your particular location—represents scarcity rent. The rest reflects the value of the building itself, the services your landlord provides, his cost of money, and other things.

The existence of scarcity rent is closely linked to the existence of private property. As Adam Smith noted, back in the days when land was the main source of rent, "As soon as the land of any country has all become private property, the landlords, like all other men, love to reap where they never sowed, and demand a rent even for its natural produce. The wood of the forest, the grass of the field, and all natural fruits of the earth, which, when land was in common, cost the labourer only the trouble of gathering them, come, even to him, to have an additional price fixed upon them. He must then pay for the license to gather them; and he must give up to the landlord a portion of what his labour either collects or produces. This portion constitutes the rent."

David Ricardo, the next great economist after Smith, was the first to note that rent could be charged for water and air, as well as for land. He wrote prophetically in 1817, "[If] air, water, the elasticity of steam, and the pressure of the atmosphere, were of various qualities; if they could be appropriated, and each quality existed only in moderate abundance, they, as well as the land, would afford a rent, as the successive qualities were brought into use."

Scarcity is of course a relative, not an absolute, thing. In absolute terms, there's still a lot of carbon storage capacity left in the sky. But relative to demand—that is, relative to the rate at which we're using it up—there's not much left. Most of us alive today, and all of our children, will live to see the practical end of it.

Let's return now to the matter of wealth. It's clear that as we continue to fill the air with fumes, we'll have less and less storage capacity left. That means, if we could sell the remaining storage capacity in a market, we'd get more money for it as it got scarcer. And because there's no cost to "produce" the sky's storage capacity, the money we'd get would be pure scarcity rent. Which is to say, pure profit.

The Era of Scarce Sky

Toward the end of the nineteenth century, there was a turning point in American history. The era of free land, or at least very cheap land, came to an end. The abundance of land, as historian Frederick Jackson Turner noted, played a vital role in shaping our nation. As long as land was free or cheap, the adventurous citizen could pick up and move to the frontier, stake a claim and build a new life. Not only did this spread European settlement westward; it also created an ethos of opportunity for all (at least among Europeans).

In historical terms, another era is now ending—the era of free sky. As long as sky was free, factories and power plants could pollute without cost, and any American could cruise to a mall and pay nothing for the sky he filled up. Now, the era of scarce sky is upon us. It has come, like the era of scarce land, because we used up a gift nature can't give more of.

In the era of scarce sky, there will, of necessity, be an *economy* of sky. As happened with once common (or public) land, atmospheric property rights will be established, prices will be charged, and money will change hands—lots of money. Because of global warming, the creation of these property rights will occur soon. Then, it's off to the races. Owners of sky will collect sky rent, and that rent will flow back into the economy just as land rent now does. The battle that's looming is over who'll collect the sky rent. My proposition is that it should go to all of us equally: one citizen, one share. The mechanism for doing this should be a trust.

I confess there's something deeply ironic here. What I'm saying is that *pollution creates wealth,* or at least a certain kind of value that markets understand. This is a difficult but important paradox to grasp. It leads to a principal argument of this book: We can use the artificial wealth created by pollution to protect and share the real wealth we've all inherited. In the following chapters I'll explain how.

Chapter 3

Selling the Sky

How can you buy or sell the sky, the warmth of the land? The idea is strange to us.

—Chief Seattle

Air, water and land are not the "free good" our society once believed. They must be redefined as assets, so that they can be efficiently and appropriately allocated.

—Frank Popoff, former CEO, Dow Chemical

1963
Lee Iacocca designs the Ford Mustang; Kennedy is assassinated.
Carbon dioxide concentration in the air: 319 parts per million
Average temperature at surface of the earth: 57.2°F

The idea of buying and selling the sky is indeed strange. Many even consider it sacrilegious. Yet, given the logic of capitalism, drawing a line and then selling a gradually declining amount of sky below that line is the best way to save it.

By the foregoing, I don't mean to suggest that the sky has no value other than its exchange value. The sky, in my mind, is a gift of cre-

33

ation, an utterly indispensable partner in sustaining earthly life. If anything we know can be called sacred, the sky is such a thing. It has much more than exchange value. It has incalculable *intrinsic* value.

The trouble is, markets have no appreciation for intrinsic value. They're blind and dumb and stunningly mindless; they do what they're programmed to do with ruthless aplomb. That wouldn't matter if we could run our lives without markets. But we can't. We need to communicate with markets because markets determine how resources are used. All our preachings and sermons will be for naught if we don't inscribe them on tablets that markets can understand.

Markets do understand a few things. They understand prices, property rights, demand, and supply. If you ask a market to determine the price of a thing someone owns, it will do so quickly and efficiently. Transactions will then follow. People who are willing and able to pay the market's price will pay it, and others won't. Supply and demand will find an equilibrium. This will happen more or less continuously.

This is a great system for managing scarcity. It's a lousy system, however, for measuring intrinsic value. In the case of the sky, the very incalculability of intrinsic value is what makes it necessary to create an artificial value markets *can* understand. This artificial value then becomes a proxy for the incalculable value. It's not the *equivalent* of the intrinsic value, nor an editorial comment on it. It's merely a proxy, a useful numerical substitute. And it's a much better proxy than the one markets currently use—namely, zero.

I acknowledge a deep irony here. To achieve the ends of Chief Seattle, we must use the means of Dow Chemical. The world has come to that, and it's sad. But it's important to remember the difference between means and ends. Selling the sky is not an end in itself. It's a means for achieving a higher end—the preservation of our planet.

Cap and Trade

Before there can be selling and buying, there must first be property rights. As economist John Dales has written, "You can only buy, sell, lease, rent, lend or borrow things that are owned; and the only things that are owned are property rights."

In our modern capitalist system, property rights can be assigned to individuals, married couples, corporations, partnerships, joint tenants, trusts, estates, mutual funds, nonprofit organizations, and governments. Property rights to a given asset can also be held *in toto* by one owner, or broken up and held by multiple owners. In other words, the possible configurations of property rights are immense; the only real limit is our imagination.

A primary function of government is to define and enforce property rights. But there are a number of valuable assets, the sky amongst them, for which property rights haven't yet been defined. The sky and its limited storage capacities are just out there, waiting to be taken. This has led to what biologist Garrett Hardin called *the tragedy of the commons*.

In a famous 1968 essay, Hardin wrote:

> The rational herdsman concludes that the only sensible course for him to pursue is to add another animal to his herd. And another. . . . But this is the conclusion reached by each and every rational herdsman sharing a commons. Therein is the tragedy . . .
>
> In a reverse way, the tragedy of the commons reappears in problems of pollution. Here it is not a question of taking something out of the commons, but of putting something in. . . . The rational man finds that his share of the cost of the wastes he discharges into the commons is less than the cost of purifying his wastes before releasing them. Since this is true for everyone, we are locked into a system of "fouling our own nest."

Hardin believed, erroneously, that destruction of a commons was an inevitable result of common ownership. What he didn't foresee was the invention of "cap-and-trade" systems.

Cap-and-trade systems begin with a Plimsoll line that says, "This is the total amount of pollution we'll allow. This is the maximum load line." Typically, that line gets lower every year, so pollution can be gradually phased down. These human-made lines translate the inherent scarcity of a commons into information markets can respond to.

The next step in a cap-and-trade system is the creation and assignment of property rights—the right to emit a certain amount of waste (for example, a ton of nitric oxide) into a commonly owned sink (such as the Los Angeles air basin) within a given time period (such as one year). These rights are created and assigned by government. They're a bit like leased parking spaces in a public garage. Whoever gets the spaces can use them, trade them, or sell them, but once the garage is full, that's it.

Cap-and-trade systems were a brilliant invention. They enable market economies to reduce nest-fouling, while letting businesses figure out the cheapest ways to do the job. For example, if a business can reduce its emissions for less than the cost of an emission permit, that's what it will do. If it can't, it will buy a permit from another company that can. The bottom line is that companies—and hence consumers—spend less to reduce pollution than they would if *every* company were required to reduce pollution individually.

Cap-and-trade systems have been used to reduce emissions of sulfur, lead, CFCs, and various local pollutants. The first cap-and-trade system to be applied on a major scale was designed to curb sulfur emissions, a cause of acid rain. Because coal comes with a fair amount of sulfur in it—and because sulfur dioxide in the air turns to sulfuric acid—smoke from power plants in the Midwest produces acid rain in New England and New York.

Sulfur emissions can be reduced in a number of ways. Low-sulfur coal can be burned, coal can be chemically cleansed before burning, scrubbers can remove sulfur dioxide while it's in the smokestacks, and utilities can switch to gas-fired power plants. All these measures, however, cost money. And as long as the price of emitting sulfur is zero, there's no reason for a business to spend that money.

In 1990, Congress passed and President George Bush signed a law requiring that, over twenty years, U.S. sulfur emissions be cut by 50 percent. To get below this Plimsoll line, the law gave coal-burning utilities a gradually declining number of sulfur emission permits to use, sell, or trade. A secondary market soon developed for these permits, and as this book is written, they're selling for about $126 a ton—a price set purely by supply and demand.

The sulfur cap-and-trade program has been highly successful. Sulfur emission reductions are well ahead of schedule, in part because utilities think the permits will rise in value and are saving them for future use or sale. Dire warnings (mostly from utilities and coal companies) that sulfur emission cuts would devastate the economy, proved wholly unfounded. Now, many people think a cap-and-trade system is the best way to reduce carbon dioxide emissions.

Another Tragedy

Cap-and-trade systems are an elegant solution to Hardin's *ecological* tragedy of the commons, but there's more to the story than this. There's also a second, oft-forgotten *economic* tragedy: the loss of the commons by the commoners. If we look back at the history of shared inheritances, we see a disturbing trend. From the English enclosures in the sixteenth through nineteenth centuries, to the takings of Native American and Hispanic lands in the United States, to the recent giveaway by Congress of broadcast spectrum, the story line is much the same. Just when a commons becomes commercially valuable, private owners figure out a way to grab it. The result is a loss of livelihood and potential income for commoners, and a growth in concentration of power and wealth.

The history of the broadcast spectrum—or, more colloquially, the airwaves—is a modern saga of lost common assets. When Guglielmo Marconi, a young Italian aristocrat, invented wireless radio in 1895, he expected the main use of his invention would be in ship-to-shore communication. Within a few decades, though, American entrepreneurs like David Sarnoff and George Westinghouse had set up hundreds of commercial radio stations, fueled by advertising. Instead of one-to-one communication, one-to-*many* broadcasting became the rage. Edgar Bergen, Jack Benny, and Bing Crosby, among others, competed for the eager ears of Americans—and the dollars of cigarette and soap makers. By 1930, *Billboard* magazine called radio "one of the biggest branches of the entertainment business."

The explosion of commercial broadcasting quickly encountered a natural scarcity. Because there are only a limited number of broadcast frequencies, radio stations were soon interfering with each other's signals. With everybody on the air, no one could be heard. To solve the problem, Congress set up a licensing system for broadcast frequencies.

Commons

The deal was this: Private broadcasters would be given, at no charge, the valuable right to use a specific frequency. In exchange, the broadcasters had to provide programming that served "the public interest, convenience and necessity." This meant, at least for a while, they had to present public issues fairly and without bias (the so-called Fairness Doctrine) and provide a minimal amount of educational programming for children.

The licensing of broadcast frequencies kept radio (and later, television) stations from disrupting each other's signals, but the pretext for giving away the frequencies became steadily less credible over the years. Broadcasting turned into an enormously profitable business increasingly owned by a few powerful networks. The Fairness Doctrine was dropped in the 1980s, paving the way for Rush Limbaugh and other overtly biased "infotainers." Educational programming became a joke (one television station claimed that *Teenage Mutant Ninja Turtles* fulfilled its educational obligation to children). Worst of all, our democracy was turned into a plutocracy, with office-seekers begging for money to pay broadcasters to communicate with voters—the same voters who, in theory, own the airwaves.

The latest episode in the made-for-TV mini-series, "The Great American Airwave Giveaway," played in 1995, when television station owners wanted to upgrade from analog to digital signals. This required a whole new set of frequencies—and Congress, obligingly, surrendered them free of charge. Senator John McCain, chairman of the Senate Commerce Committee, called this a $70 billion giveaway. Other conservatives agreed (see Figure 4). Even Bob Dole, the dour Republican Senate leader, was embarrassed. "It makes no sense to me that Congress would create a giant corporate welfare program when we are reforming welfare for those trapped in a failed system," Dole intoned. "The bottom line is that the spectrum is just as much a national resource as our national forests. That means it belongs to every American equally. No more, no less."

How Much Is the Sky Worth?

As a reporter in Washington in the 1960s, I had the privilege of attending the Ev and Gerry Show, a weekly press briefing conducted by Senate Republican leader Everett Dirksen and his House counterpart, Gerry

---

**WHAT CONSERVATIVES SAID
ABOUT THE $70 BILLION SPECTRUM GIVEAWAY**

"A giant corporate welfare program."
—Bob Dole

"A rip-off vaster than dreamed of by yesteryear's robber barons."
—William Safire

"A sell-out of massive proportions."
—Adam Thierer, Heritage Foundation

"Unconscionable!"
—Senator John McCain

Figure 4

Ford. Gerry, as we all know, was an amiable politician who later ascended to the presidency thanks to Watergate. Ev was a punctilious smooth-talker who now has a Senate office building named after him.

Dirksen had a wry way of putting things. When discussing a minor appropriations bill, he once said, "A billion here, a billion there—pretty soon you're talking about real money."

Well, I'm talking about real money now, too.

A 1997 study by economist Robert Costanza and others, published in the journal *Nature*, estimated the current economic value of seventeen ecosystem services at $33 *trillion* a year—a figure that exceeds the entire world's Gross Domestic Product. Moreover, that value is rising as ecosystems become stressed and scarce.

What's an ecosystem service? It's an economically valuable service that nature provides to humans. For example, nature gives us water, seafood, timber, natural fibers, and many pharmaceuticals—that is, actual goods we consume. In addition, nature performs many services we scarcely notice. It purifies air and water, detoxifies and decomposes wastes, disperses seeds and nutrients, pollinates crops, and regulates climate.

The invisibility of nature's services is one reason we find Costanza's numbers so astonishing. As Gretchen Daily has written,

> If asked to identify all that goes into making a fine cake, a baker would probably identify its ingredients, and the skill required to transform them into a culinary work of art. She might also describe the oven, pan and kitchen gadgets needed. If pressed further, she might point out the need for capital infrastructure and human services to process, store, and transport the ingredients. However, the chances of the baker touching directly upon the natural renewal of soil fertility, the pollination of crops, natural pest control, the role of biodiversity in maintaining crop productivity—or, indeed, upon any ecosystem service involved—are extremely remote. Ecosystem services are absolutely essential to civilization, but modern life obscures their existence.

How did Costanza and his colleagues come up with their numbers? They used a variety of techniques only sophisticated economists understand. And perhaps they're off by a few trillion. But here's the point: The conclusion to be drawn from Costanza's work is that *commonly inherited gifts of nature provide more (or at least a comparable amount of) wealth to humanity than all human efforts combined.*

This is a rather humbling thought. As an entrepreneur, I used to believe that people like me were the primary creators of wealth. Yet, as it turns out, even Bill Gates is a piker when compared to Mother Nature.

There's another conclusion to be drawn from Costanza's paper: *A market system that values such an enormous trove of wealth at exactly zero is fundamentally flawed.* This is like the failure of cosmologists to account for 90 percent of the mass of the universe. It's as if markets have managed to lose track of most of economic reality.

This is a serious problem. As I've noted earlier, the failure of markets to put a proper price on nature is causing a steady deterioration of our inherited wealth. We're devouring our natural capital and imagining we're richer. We think we're leaving a better world for our children, when in fact we're leaving them poorer.

What to do? I concur with Frank Popoff, former CEO of Dow Chemical: *Redefine our air, water, and other ecosystems as assets,* so companies like Dow will respect them. If, for example, we made the sky into an asset, chemical companies (and everyone else) would pay a price to use it. The price would be set by markets based on supply and demand. As supply gets scarcer, the price will rise. This "exchange value" will never equal the sky's intrinsic value. But it *will* be a price much greater than zero, and a cost Dow Chemical will understand.

What might that price be? The carbon storage capacity of the sky wasn't one of the services measured by Costanza, so we must look elsewhere. Fortunately, several recent studies have estimated the future price of carbon storage capacity. These studies make assumptions about future demand for carbon, the rate at which energy technologies may change, and the timing and level of future carbon emission caps. After plugging these assumptions into computer models of the U.S. economy, they come up with some numbers. These numbers represent the scarcity rent that users of the sky will pay for its limited carbon absorption capacity.

And the numbers are big. For example, DRI/McGraw-Hill, a leading consulting firm, has estimated that the sale of carbon emission permits could generate $140 billion to $280 billion a year starting in 2010. The Energy Information Administration of the U.S. government, making comparable assumptions, came up with an estimate of $386 billion. That's not $386 billion *once,* it's that amount *every year* for many years. The driving factor in all these estimates is scarcity—that is, the lower the quantity of emission permits, the more money they'll fetch. That's the less-is-more magic of scarcity rent.

As Everett Dirksen might have said, a hundred billion here, a hundred billion there—pretty soon you're talking about $1,000 per American woman, man, and child, year after year. And that's real pie in the sky.

Why Not Tax Nature?

Some economists say, "Why go to the trouble of creating property rights for nature? Why not just tax it?" The effect, they argue, will be the same: People will have to pay for using the atmosphere, say, and that will discourage them from using it. This was, for a while, the party line at Redefining Progress.

Well, maybe. The idea of using taxes to discourage pollution was first suggested in 1920 by Arthur Pigou, the top economist at Cambridge University. Eighty years later, though the idea has made little progress in the real world, it's acquired cachet in academic circles. The analogy that's often made is to "sin" taxes such as those on alcohol and tobacco. Presumably, these discourage drinking and smoking.

I'm skeptical of so-called Pigovian taxes for several reasons. The first is ecological—I don't think we'll ever cut carbon emissions by 90 percent (or even 50 percent) just by taxing them. Our industrial economy's attachment to carbon is in many ways analogous to an addiction. Just as individuals addicted to nicotine or alcohol won't break their habits just because the price goes up, so nothing short of actual supply limits will cause us to break our collective carbon habit.

My second reason for skepticism is the sheer improbability of doing it right. Consider what's implied by the Pigovian vision. First, economists will have to calculate what just the right tax is to reduce carbon emissions by a desired amount. The odds that economists will agree on any number—much less that it will be the *right* number—are exceedingly low. Even if they agree on a number that is, miraculously, the right one, they'll still have to persuade Congress to adopt it.

Now, Congress is an ornery body that harbors a broad diversity of views on the subject of taxation—and is not unswayed by campaign contributors. The likelihood that this body and the President will accept the wise tax advice of economists is not great. More likely, Congress will adopt the wrong number, and the desired drop in emissions won't be reached. What then happens?

Presumably, economists will go back to their computers and the whole process will start again. Maybe Congress will come closer to the "right" tax the next time. Most likely, it will miss again and another round will be required. The Soviet Union had a system like this. Prices were set by bureaucrats and commissars, and it didn't work very well. There's a reason why, in America, we let markets, not politicians, set prices.

My third concern is this: Carbon taxes, even if offset by cuts in other taxes, will redistribute income the wrong way. Like all consumption taxes, carbon taxes would impose the heaviest burden on those who can least afford them. The higher energy prices poor people would pay could not easily be offset by other tax reductions.

The idea that there's another way to charge for externalities—a way involving property rights rather than taxes—dates back to the 1950s. Its originator was another scholarly Briton, Ronald Coase, who studied at the London School of Economics in the 1930s and emigrated to the United States after World War II.

Coase was an obscure academic until one fateful night in 1958. The *Journal of Law and Economics,* based at the University of Chicago, had invited Coase to discuss his ideas at dinner—along with Milton Friedman and about twenty other luminaries. When the evening began, one participant recalls, the line-up against Coase was 20 to 1. Then, Milton Friedman opened fire and the bullets hit everyone but Coase. By the end of the evening, Coase had converted the house.

Coase argued that pollution can be reduced by assigning property rights. For example, polluters could be given the right to pollute, or pollut*ees* could be given the right *not* to be polluted. Either way, a market in pollution rights would emerge, and less pollution would result.

Think about it this way. If polluters got the initial rights, pollutees could band together (assuming they had knowledge of the pollution) and pay the polluters not to pollute, since it's worth something to the pollutees not to be polluted. Conversely, if pollut*ees* got the initial rights, pollut*ers* might pay them for the right to pollute in order to avoid the costs of abating pollution. Eventually, markets would work out a level of pollution and money exchange acceptable to both sides. This, by definition, would be the "optimum" level of pollution.

There is, Coase admitted, one caveat: The model only works if transaction costs are low. For example, if pollutees must rely on costly law suits to recover damages from polluters, it won't work.

The Chicagoans, despite their libertarian bent, were stunned. They'd gone to dinner believing, along with liberals, that government could do certain things better than markets, and that controlling pollution was one of those things. They went home with a vision of less government and more property rights. Swiftly, they lured Coase to Chicago as editor of the *Journal of Law and Economics,* and launched a line of thinking that led to the cap-and-trade systems I described earlier. Thirty-three years later, Coase was awarded a Nobel Prize.

I like Coase's thinking a lot, except for one thing—the strange indifference to equity at its heart. To Coase *it made no difference who got the initial property rights.* Assuming low transaction costs, the result as he saw it was the same: less pollution.

In the real world, of course, it makes a huge difference who gets property rights. An initial recipient of property rights receives a gift of wealth and power. Moreover, as University of California economist Mason Gaffney has written, "Entitlements—the initial assignments of property rights—have a major effect on the relative bargaining power of different parties. If you don't think entitlements matter, give them to me. Then let's talk."

To me, Coase's model is ideal *if* the initial property rights are given to the pollutees—that is, in the case of carbon dioxide, to everyone. If that's done, I'd happily forget pollution taxes and other forms of pollution control. Just draw a Plimsoll line, I'd say, and sell the sky. Yes, go ahead and sell it. Let markets set the price, and pay the proceeds to the rightful owners—you, me, and our children.

Chapter 4

Who Owns the Sky?

Blessed are the meek, for they shall inherit the earth.
—Jesus of Nazareth

1973
First OPEC oil price jolt; Watergate simmers.
Carbon dioxide concentration in the air: 329 parts per million
Average temperature at surface of the earth: 57.5°F

Could this be the century when the meek actually *do* inherit the earth—or at least part of it? This possibility exists. Because new property rights (thanks to new scarcities) must be created, Congress must choose *someone* to own them. There's thus a rare historical opportunity to fulfill an ancient prophecy.

Who owns—or should own—the sky? In the coming era of scarce sky, the answer will affect every American's pocketbook. The answer will determine to whom we and our children—and every generation of Americans thereafter—pay sky rent. It's nothing less than a trillion-dollar question.

It's also a question rich in religious, philosophic, and legal overtones. It taps into age-old preachings of the Prophets, centuries-old traditions of the commons, and some of the oldest political debates in America. And it's a global question as well, since Americans aren't the only ones who use the sky.

Indian journalist Sunita Narain once asked me, "How can *any* American claim a right to the sky, when you've already used more than your share?" Her point is well taken. Roughly half the excess carbon dioxide in the sky today was put there by Americans. Now, developing countries want most of what carbon storage capacity is left. They say the sky's remaining carbon storage capacity should be allocated on a per capita basis. The United States, not surprisingly, says it should be based on historic emissions. A compromise has yet to be reached.

In this book I assume the United States will have *some* chunk of the global atmosphere, and that we'll decide among ourselves how that chunk will be allocated domestically. I also distinguish between *use* of the sky and *beneficial ownership* of it. In a cap-and-trade system, the right to *use* the sky is linked to ownership of emission permits that can be freely bought and sold. The right to the economic benefit from the sky—that is, to receive the income derived from users of the sky—is something else. Henceforth, it's this right I'll be talking about. In real estate terms, it's like the landlord's right to collect rent from tenants.

In pondering the question of who is, or should be, the beneficial owner of America's chunk of sky, a good place to start is with Roman law, from which our system of property rights evolved. Roman law distinguished between four types of property.

- *Res privatæ,* private things—things in the possession of an individual or corporation.

- *Res publicæ,* public things—things owned and set aside for public use by the government, such as public buildings, highways and navigable waterways.

- *Res communes,* common things—things accessible to all that can't be exclusively possessed by an individual or government.

- *Res nullius,* unowned things—things that have no property rights attached until they're taken into possession and become *res privatæ* or *res publicæ*.

Like Roman law, English law distinguished between two kinds of public property, one belonging to the state and the other to all citizens. The Magna Carta, signed in 1215, established fisheries as a *res communes*, a commons available to all. (Prior to the Magna Carta, the king could grant exclusive fishing rights.) Similar status was given to the air, running water, and wild animals. There's thus an old and clear distinction between common property and state property, and the air falls decidedly into the common category.

England added the institution of land owned in common by villagers. Such common lands could be used for growing crops, grazing animals, and collecting wood, so they were more than wild nature—they were a source of sustenance and income. They were distinct from common areas open to all people; they were a kind of community asset, open only to members of the village.

In the New World, many early settlements also had common lands (the Boston Commons was once a shared sheep pasture). Further, the old distinction between *res communes* and *res publicæ* was kept alive in a judicial concept known as the public trust doctrine. This doctrine says that while legal title to rivers, shorelines, and the air might reside in the state, the state merely holds them "in trust" for the people, who are their beneficial owners. A few state constitutions say this explicitly. Thus, "All public natural resources are held in trust by the State for the benefit of the People," declares Hawaii's constitution.

The U.S. Supreme Court has upheld the public trust doctrine on numerous occasions. Says University of Texas law professor Gerald Torres: "The beneficial interest in any *res communes* is held by the people in common. The state does not own a river or the sky like it owns the furniture in the state house. The power of the government to divest the people of their common interest is limited. Even where such a divestiture is justified, the proceeds of that transaction belong to the people."

There's a deeper philosophical question here, too—one that runs like a long thread through the fabric of American history: Who takes precedence, the people or the government? According to John Locke, the philosopher who most influenced America's founders, people at first existed in a state of nature in which there was no formal government. Later, governments were formed (and tolerated) because they provided services and protections individuals couldn't get on their own.

Locke's ideas were incorporated in the Declaration of Independence, which proclaimed that (1) "Governments are instituted among Men (sic)" to secure inalienable rights; (2) governments derive "their just powers from the consent of the governed"; and (3) "whenever any Form of Government becomes destructive of these ends, it is the Right of the People to alter or to abolish it."

The idea that "we, the people" create government for our own purposes is also embodied in the U.S. Constitution of 1789, which begins:

> We the People of the United States, in Order to form a more perfect Union, establish Justice, insure domestic Tranquility, provide for the common defence, promote the general Welfare, and secure the Blessings of Liberty to ourselves and our Posterity, do ordain and establish this Constitution for the United States of America.

This notion was reinforced in the Tenth Amendment, which at James Madison's behest was added to the Constitution to allay fears the federal government might grow too powerful: "The powers not delegated to the United States by the Constitution, nor prohibited by it to the States, are reserved to the States respectively, or to the people." And it was restated four score years later when an embattled Abraham Lincoln vowed to preserve government "of the people, by the people and for the people."

These lofty historical pronouncements can of course be set aside as ancient rhetoric, with little relevance to the twenty-first century. But as a thought experiment, let's imagine taking them seriously. Let's suppose that we, the people, precede government, and that what isn't explicitly granted to the government belongs to the people. The question this line of thinking raises is, Is the notion of ownership by "the people," as opposed to ownership by the state, too abstract to have any practical meaning? Or is there a mechanism by which assets such as the sky can in fact be beneficially owned by "the people"? Happily, the answer to the second question is yes.

Three Candidates

Practically speaking, there are three possible beneficial owners of America's chunk of the sky: private corporations, the federal government, and citizens through a nationwide trust.

Corporate ownership isn't as far-fetched as it might seem. U.S. history has been marked by numerous giveaways of common assets to private corporations, from the enormous land grants to railroads in the nineteenth century to the recent gift of spectrum to broadcasters. The standard argument used to justify such largesse is that, in exchange for common assets, the receiving corporations deliver a *quid pro quo* of public value: They build railroads, extract valuable minerals, or transmit sharper TV images. The public thus gets a return on its in-kind investment, making the deals at least arguably fair.

Whether past in-kind investments of this sort were good deals for the public is debatable. If measured by the rigorous yardsticks of Wall Street, most probably weren't. (Are sharper TV pictures worth $70 billion?) But there's no doubt a future gift of carbon storage capacity to private corporations would be a terrible investment. There's *nothing* we'd get in return. Such a gift would be a pure handout, like giving away offshore oil for free. I've heard only one plausible justification for doing this: It might win political support, or at least acquiescence, from energy companies for carbon emission reductions. In other words, it would be a political payoff.

The argument for *federal* ownership of carbon absorption capacity is stronger than the case for corporate ownership. Presumably, the federal government represents the public interest, and therefore its ownership of the sky would, *ipso facto,* serve the public interest. This presumption, however, is arguable. If we look at the historical record, it's not at all clear that the federal government has managed common assets in the public interest. Quite to the contrary, it has all too often disposed of valuable common assets (land, minerals, timber, water, and spectrum) at far below market value.

The reason for such poor stewardship isn't hard to uncover. Like any political body, the federal government is subject to pressure from private interests who stand to gain from use of common assets. Though in theory the federal government defends the interests of all citizens, and of future as well as present generations, in practice it caters to private interests who want favors *now.*

Even if the government *did* receive fair market value for carbon storage capacity, that would solve only half the problem. While the right amount of sky rent would go *into* the U.S. Treasury, there'd be no assurance it would come *out*—or if it did, who would get it. In the end, the argument for federal ownership of the sky rests mostly on lack of imagination ("there's no other way to do it"). But Alaska has shown there *is* another way—a modern form of common ownership. I believe it's a better way than federal ownership.

North to Alaska!

Jay Hammond is an unlikely herald of a new economic era. Born in Troy, New York, in 1922, a Methodist minister's son, he was for many years an outdoor adventurer and bush pilot. Moving to Alaska after World War II, he settled in the treeless, windswept fishing village of Naknek. In 1959, a couple of friends talked him into running for the state legislature. Despite the fact that he was a white Republican in an overwhelmingly Native and Democratic district—not to mention the fact that he didn't campaign at all—Hammond won. Thus began an accidental political career that ended with eight years in the governor's mansion.

While in Naknek, Hammond noticed that most of the wealth from the local fishery was reaped by outsiders. Billions of dollars were being extracted, while coastal communities remained little more than slums.

To capture some of that lost wealth, Hammond tried to get his borough to enact a 3 percent tax on fish. Even though outsiders would pay almost the entire tax, residents voted it down twice. Finally Hammond found the winning formula. He tied the fish tax to an elimination of local property taxes, and this time voters went for it. Soon roads and schools were built, and *Fortune* magazine described the borough as "the richest municipality in the nation" in terms of per capita revenue.

The experience got Hammond thinking about how to share other gifts of nature. Several years later, when he was governor, oil started flowing from Prudhoe Bay. Fortuitously, the wells were located on land that had been granted to the state by the federal government. This meant Alaska would be rich—especially since OPEC had just pushed oil prices sky-high. The question was, what should the state do with its windfall?

Some Alaskans wanted to spend it on big public works projects. Hammond, being fiscally conservative, opposed this. Noting that, under the Alaska Constitution, the natural resources of the state belong to its people, he proposed a dividend-paying investment fund in which all Alaskans would be shareholders. He called it "Alaska, Inc."

In Hammond's original plan, Alaska, Inc. would receive half the state's oil revenue. This would be invested in a portfolio of stocks and bonds that would outlive Prudhoe Bay's oil supply. Annual earnings from this portfolio would again be divided in half. Fifty percent would go for schools, highways, and other infrastructure. The rest would be paid out in dividends to shareholders. Children's dividends would be held in interest-bearing accounts until they reached age eighteen.

Hammond argued that "each Alaskan—not the politicians—should decide how to spend some of the resource wealth each owned." Hot political battles ensued. When the dust finally settled, Alaskans had amended their state constitution to create what was called the Alaska Permanent Fund, separate from the state legislature. The Permanent Fund was close to Hammond's idea of Alaska, Inc. The chief difference was

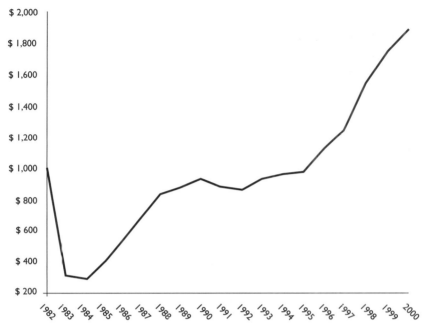

Figure 5. Alaska's Dividends
Alaska's citizens receive dividends from the Alaska Permanent Fund. The Fund's earnings are divided equally every year among all state residents and have grown steadily for the past sixteen years.
Source: Alaska Permanent Fund <www.apfc.org>.

that only 25 percent of the state's oil revenue went into the fund. A key provision was that the state legislature could not touch money in the Permanent Fund without approval by the voters.

Interestingly, in the initial version of the Permanent Fund, the distribution of shares would not have been equal. All Alaskans would have received shares under a formula based on years of residency since statehood. Old timers would have received more shares than newcomers. This provision was challenged in a lawsuit brought by attorneys Ron and Penny Zobel, who argued that the residency-based formula unconstitutionally discriminated against newcomers like themselves. The case went all the way to the U.S. Supreme Court. In 1982 the high Court ruled that the unequal dividend formula did indeed violate the Equal Protection

Clause of the Fourteenth Amendment, and ordered Alaska to make its dividends equal.

As soon as this change was made, the Permanent Fund began writing checks. The first dividend was $1,000, an amount that reflected income that had built up while the Supreme Court case was being argued. In 1984 the dividend dropped to $331, and since then it has steadily risen to $1,964. If you look around the world at other oil-rich states—from Saudi Arabia to Texas—a strong case can be made that none has handled its oil wealth better than Alaska.

Today the Alaska Permanent Fund operates out of a small office in Juneau. It has thirty-two employees and a six-person board of trustees appointed by the governor. It manages a portfolio worth over $27 billion, making it one of the hundred largest investment funds in the world. Its official mission is "to produce income to benefit all generations of Alaskans." Alaskans proudly view it as a well-managed common savings account. When state legislators tried to raid the Fund in 1999 to offset a budget deficit, voters in a referendum stopped them by 83 to 17 percent. The voters' message was clear: Don't touch our money! (For more information about the Alaska Permanent Fund, visit its excellent Web site <www.apfc.org>.)

The State Is Not the Commons

My proposal can be boiled down to this: What Alaska did with oil, the whole country should do with sky. Like Alaskans in the 1970s, we're about to inherit a windfall. Theirs came from under the ground, ours comes from above. Theirs was worth billions, ours is worth trillions.

Why is Alaska-style citizen ownership of the sky preferable to ownership by the federal government? There are several reasons in my mind. One is essentially religious. It rests on a belief that the sky is a gift from our common creator. It wasn't given to a government, and certainly not to private corporations. We, the meek, are its inheritors. If it turns out this gift is worth real money, well, that money belongs to us and our heirs. (Incidentally, Jesus' beatitude derives from the Old Testament's

Psalm 37: "But the meek shall inherit the land and shall delight in abundant prosperity.")

A second reason has to do with values and priorities. Federal ownership of the sky would strengthen the apparatus of the state; citizen ownership would strengthen families and children. If we truly believe that families and children are the bedrock of our society, we should design our institutions and allocate our resources accordingly.

A third reason is this: The sky is nothing if not the ultimate commons. We all inhale oxygen from it, exhale carbon dioxide into it, and use it daily in many other ways. On the theory that use implies ownership, or simply that commoners own the commons, the sky should be our common property.

In my view, what inhibits Americans from creating an Alaska-style trust for the sky is a confusion between the commons and the state. They're often considered to be the same, when in fact they're not. Historically, the English commons were owned by the commoners who used them. State property—the king's property—was something else. When the commons were enclosed, the land went not to the king or to the state, but to the local gentry. The commoners' ownership interest was acknowledged with small cash payments.

Conceivably, the federal government could own the sky *on behalf of the people*—that is, as trustee of the people's asset. The trouble is, this type of arrangement hasn't worked well in the past. Even when the federal government has been explicitly designated as a trustee—as with the spectrum, our national forests, and numerous Native American lands— it has done a less than exemplary job.

For example, the U.S. Forest Service is in charge of 192 million acres. For most of the twentieth century, it focused on production of timber and minerals rather than ecosystem conservation. Consequently, the national forests have been scarred by logging roads, clear-cuts, stream sedimentation, and mining wastes. Adding insult to injury is the fact that taxpayers have subsidized this destruction. The Forest Service has spent billions of dollars on logging roads so private companies can harvest our trees, and has then sold these trees at below-market prices. If the Forest Service had been a business, it would have gone bankrupt long ago.

Another sorry example involves the Interior and Treasury Departments. For over a century they've been in charge of trust funds set up for the benefit of hundreds of thousands of Native Americans. These accounts, known as Individual Indian Money Trusts, were intended to compensate the Indians for use of their land. Royalties from petroleum, timber, and other resources were supposed to be paid to the account-holders, many of whom are desperately poor. In 1996, the Native American Rights Fund filed a lawsuit alleging that the government had so badly managed the accounts that recipients had lost billions of dollars. The federal judge hearing the case found the evidence "overwhelming" that the government had failed to perform its fiduciary duties. Citing Interior Secretary Bruce Babbitt and Treasury Secretary Robert Rubin for contempt, the judge ordered them to clean up the hundred-year-old mess as quickly as possible.

Perhaps the federal government simply has too many things to do. Perhaps it's so big and distant that citizens can't stay on top of what it's doing (though inside-the-Beltway lobbyists clearly can). Or perhaps it's under the heel of special interests like timber, mining, and oil companies. Whatever the reasons, the federal government has had two hundred years to prove its *bona fides* as a trustee, and has failed to do so. Is it unreasonable now to seek an alternative?

Twenty-First Century Common Ownership

Never let it be said that Americans can't invent financial instruments to do *anything*. Flip through the *Wall Street Journal* and you'll find, amidst two dozen pages of stock listings, a menagerie of financial creations that rivals Dr. Seuss in off-beat zaniness. There are Fannie Maes and Freddie Macs, pork belly and palladium futures, yen and Euro futures options, corporate junk bonds, California electricity at the Oregon border, NAS-DAQ 100 index options, and a veritable zoo of other derivatives. They're all traded daily in such places as the New York Futures Exchange, the New York Mercantile Exchange, and the Chicago Board of Trade. Though I'm sure they all serve useful purposes, I'd be hard-pressed to tell you what those are. Nevertheless, the great variety of derivatives makes me highly confident that Yankee ingenuity can structure common ownership of the sky.

Two instruments are needed to turn the sky into an income-producing asset for all Americans. The first is *tradeable carbon emission permits*. These are similar to the sulfur emission permits that already exist. They'd be sold at least annually to companies that bring fossil fuels into the U.S. economy—Exxon-Mobil, Peabody Coal, El Paso

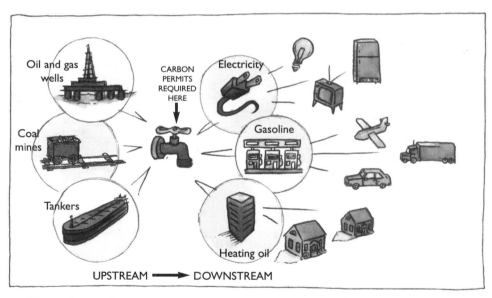

Figure 6. Cranking Down Carbon at the Source
An upstream permit system would act like a spigot at the place where carbon enters the U.S. economy. The spigot would be gradually cranked down by reducing the number of permits. Such an upstream permit system would limit all *carbon in the economy and be much easier to administer than a downstream system.*

Natural Gas, and about two thousand others. Each permit would represent the right to store one ton of carbon in America's share of the global atmosphere. These permits would be "attached" to carbon as it leaves the coal mine, oil or gas well, or shipping port. The reason for attaching the permits here is that it's a lot easier to keep tabs on carbon at the beginning of its journey through the economy than at the end, when it's coming out of millions of tailpipes, smokestacks, and chimneys.

Companies at the top of the carbon chain would buy and sell carbon emission permits to suit their needs. On December 31 of each year, they'd have to own enough permits to cover all the emittable carbon they brought into the economy during the preceding year. If they didn't, they'd be penalized. No emissions monitoring would be required—just financial reporting similar to what the companies already provide to a variety of government agencies.

Bear in mind that this kind of permit selling would differ from the sales of spectrum frequencies that occurred occasionally in the 1990s. Once a spectrum frequency is sold, it's sold forever. The government gets a one-time payment, and that's it. Carbon emission permits would be more like rentals. You'd get the right to emit a ton of carbon this year, but if you want to emit another ton next year, you'd have to buy another permit. The revenue from selling carbon emission permits would thus continue indefinitely.

It's also worth noting that this carbon permiting system would differ from the existing sulfur system in two important ways. First, the carbon emission permits would be sold rather than given away, or "grandfathered," to historic polluters. This is important because the scarcity rent associated with carbon is roughly a hundred times greater than the scarcity rent associated with sulfur. The second difference is that while sulfur permits must be owned by the end users—the actual emitters—carbon permits would be owned by the *first* users—the companies that introduce carbon into the economy. In technical lingo, the sulfur permits are *downstream* while the carbon permits would be

ım permits have several advantages. First, you catch *all* the carbon that enters the economy (and eventually, the sky); any down-stream system will inevitably leave many holes unplugged. Second, you make life simpler all around. Only a few thousand firms would need to own upstream carbon permits; in a downstream system, nearly everyone would. And in an upstream system, you don't have to monitor every smokestack and tailpipe (a hopeless task). You need only know the quantities of coal, oil, and natural gas that pass through the upstream companies—information that's readily available.

In effect, establishing an upstream carbon permit system would be like putting a spigot at the place where carbon enters the economy. That spigot could then be turned down gradually, by a few percentage points a year, until we reach a tolerable level of carbon burning.

The second instrument needed to turn the sky into an income-producing asset for all Americans is a dividend-paying trust, similar to the Alaska Permanent Fund. Wall Street's wizards could design this entity in a New York minute. I'd name it the U.S. Sky Trust.

In many ways, the Sky Trust reminds me of my early days at Working Assets. Our first product was the Working Assets Money Fund. Except for its social investing criteria, this was a plain-vanilla mutual fund. It was organized as a trust in Massachusetts. It had a nine-person board of trustees initially appointed by the founders and subsequently elected by the shareholders. The trustees were accountable directly to the shareholders. They hired a management company to run the fund, and had the power to fire that company if it didn't perform. Major policy changes had to be approved by a majority vote of shareholders.

The main difference between the Sky Trust and an ordinary mutual fund—aside from their different assets—lies in the nature of their shares. A mutual fund's shares can be bought and sold any day of the week, and there's no limit on how many shares you can own. More money buys you more shares. A Sky Trust share, by contrast, could not be bought or sold, and you could only own one. It would be a non-transferable birthright that's part of your citizenship package. When you become a U.S. citizen, whether by birth or naturalization, you'd get one vote, the obligation to serve on juries, and one Sky Trust share. When you die, your Sky Trust share would die with you, just as your vote does.

In the next chapter, I describe how this Sky Trust could work. Then, in the three following, I discuss its long-term implications.

Chapter 5

How a Sky Trust Would Work

A good man leaves an inheritance to his children's children.

—Proverbs (13:22)

A spoonful of sugar helps the medicine go down.

—Mary Poppins

1980
Acid rain mounts; Reagan is elected.
Carbon dioxide concentration in the air: 339 parts per million
Average temperature at surface of the earth: 57.7°F

One of my jobs at Working Assets was to develop new products. It's a tricky job, more art than science. In an earlier chapter I told you about my successes; I didn't mention my numerous failures.

A product developer has to imagine a whole range of things: What the product will look like, what benefit it will provide, who it will appeal to, what it will cost, how it will be produced, marketed, distributed, and so on. S/he has to do this one step at a time, starting with a "big idea" and then refining it again and again until all the pieces fit together.

Over the years I acquired a few biases in designing new products. One is that they should be of enduring value—the customer should continue to enjoy them year after year. Another is that they should be customer-friendly—they should be easy to use and leave you with a good feeling. The Sky Trust meets these tests. In my view, it's a product waiting to be launched.

The idea of a Sky Trust first came to me in 1995, when I was a senior fellow at Redefining Progress. At RP, I explored such seemingly disparate problems as the aging of our population and global warming. One day it hit me: The carbon storage capacity of the sky is a very valuable asset. But whose asset is it? I didn't see anyone around who owned it—who, as an owner, could limit usage and charge prices. Maybe we needed to find an owner, I thought. But who might that be?

In the years since then, the initial idea—that the sky is a valuable asset and ought to have an appropriate owner—has gone through numerous refinements. It gestated at the Corporation for Enterprise Development and, independently, at Resources for the Future, two centrist think tanks. It was presented at numerous briefings, examined and tweaked by experts, and floated in the corridors of power. The result is what we now call the Sky Trust.

Just to review a bit, the Sky Trust is one of three possible kinds of cap-and-trade systems. In one kind, the initial emission rights are given to historic polluters for free. In a second kind, the initial emission rights are sold to polluters by the government, which uses the revenue as it sees fit. In the third kind, the initial emission rights are given to a trust, which periodically sells them to polluters and distributes the revenue to all citizens equally.

The Sky Trust is a cap-and-trade system of this last kind. You can look at it as both a civic institution and as a mechanism for recycling scarcity rent. As a civic institution, it would embody our common ownership of a shared inheritance. Because of my business background, I sometimes think of it as a kind of mutual fund. Like all mutual funds, it would be owned by its shareholders and distribute its income equally per share. What would differentiate it from standard mutual funds are the nature of

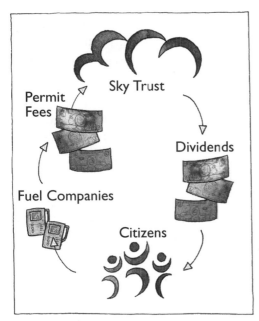

Figure 7. The Sky Trust Working
A Sky Trust would be a scarcity rent recycling machine. As consumers, citizens would pay more for burning fossil fuels, but as owners, they'd get yearly dividends. Those who burn more carbon would lose money; those who burn less carbon would come out ahead.

its shares—one per citizen, nontransferable—and its responsibility to future as well as current shareholders.

The key protections I'd build into the Sky Trust as a civic institution are *transparency* and *accountability.* By transparency, I mean that citizens should be able to see where every dollar comes from and goes. Thus, there'd be no co-mingling of sky income with other funds. Shareholders would receive an audited annual report with complete financial information. And this information would be instantly available on the World Wide Web.

Accountability would also be built into the legal structure of the Sky Trust, just as it is for other trusts. Unlike corporations, trusts have long-term missions that their trustees are legally bound to fulfill. If they deviate from their long-term mission, the trustees can be sued by beneficiaries. In some cases, trustees are elected by beneficiaries.

The Sky Trust's mission would be to preserve the mix of gases in the sky. Its trustees would be accountable not only to citizens alive today, but also to citizens yet unborn. They'd have three legal responsibilities: (1) to issue carbon burning permits up to a limit established by Congress; (2) to receive market prices for those permits; and (3) to distribute the income equally. These responsibilities, as it turns out, are consistent to a remarkable degree. In the event there *were* a conflict between the trustees' responsibilities, preservation of the sky would take precedence.

The other way to view the Sky Trust is as a scarcity rent recycling machine. We, the users, pay scarcity rent for the sky because—well, because it's scarce. We, the owners, then get back our share of the scarcity rent because—well, because we're the owners. In terms of total money in and total money out, the whole thing's a wash. But for you, me, and millions of other individual citizens, the recycling of scarcity rent can make a big difference.

Why does recycling scarcity rent matter? Keep in mind this fact: If carbon emissions are limited, we as consumers will pay higher prices *whether or not there's rent recycling.* That's because the mere act of limiting carbon emissions will create scarcity rent, which will show up in higher prices. Think of it this way. If carbon emissions are limited, the effect is the same as limiting the supply of fossil fuels. That's what OPEC did in the 1970s, and you know what happened. Without rent recycling, the higher prices from limiting carbon emissions would be a windfall for oil companies and their shareholders. *With* rent recycling we'd return the windfall to its rightful owners—ourselves.

Also remember this: Though everyone will *receive* an equal share of scarcity rent from the Sky Trust, not everyone will *pay* the same amount. Those who burn more carbon will pay more than those who burn less. If you drive a sports utility vehicle, you'll use more sky than if you ride a bus; hence you'll pay more scarcity rent. Since your dividend is the same no matter what, you'll come out ahead if you conserve, and lose money if you don't. In other words, money will flow from overusers of the sky to underusers. Economizers will be rewarded, squanderers will pay. This isn't only fair; it's precisely the right incentive to reduce pollution.

From this perspective, the U.S. Sky Trust is different from the Alaska Permanent Fund. The Permanent Fund's initial revenue comes from sale of oil to non-Alaskans, while dividends flow entirely to Alaskans. Thus, all Alaskans gain. The Sky Trust's money, by contrast, would come from and go to roughly the same people: us. Whether you, as an individual, come out ahead or behind would depend on how much carbon you burn.

As it turns out, the Sky Trust's shifting of money from high- to low-carbon burners favors families with lower incomes. That's because poor families tend not to drive big cars, occupy big homes, or fly around the world in jets. A study by economist Marc Breslow confirms this. Using Census Bureau and other government figures, Breslow found that if you rank U.S. households by income, the bottom 60 percent would gain money with a Sky Trust, while the top 40 percent would lose. A similar study by the Congressional Budget Office found that the bottom 40 percent would gain, the top 40 percent would lose, and the middle 20 percent would roughly break even. By contrast, if carbon emissions are reduced *without* recycling the scarcity rent, all but the top 20 percent would *lose*. Wealthy households would gain because, as stockholders, they'd share in the windfall that energy companies would reap if carbon permits are given away to historic emitters.

The Sky Trust has several other features worth noting. Because it pays dividends on a per capita basis, and includes children and stay-at-home parents among its beneficiaries, the Sky Trust is a pro-family institution. A family of four with one breadwinner would get four times as much as a single person. Moreover, in the version proposed by the Corporation for Enterprise Development, parents could put their children's dividends into tax-free Individual Development Accounts. These savings would be invested by the family and could be expected to grow over time. Eventually, the money could be used by the grown children for higher education, vocational training, first home purchase, or starting a small business. In effect, every American child would have a trust fund managed by his/her parents.

Another important feature of the Sky Trust is its Transition Fund. There's no doubt that higher carbon prices will hurt some families and communities more than others. Many of America's coal miners will lose their jobs. Farmers and truckers who drive long distances will also be hurt, as will poor people in cold climes whose winter heating bills soar. To help those who are most hurt by higher carbon prices, the Sky Trust includes a ten-year Transition Fund. In its first year of operation, 25 percent of the Sky Trust's revenues would flow into this fund; the remaining 75 percent would go for dividends. Thereafter, the Transition Fund's share of revenue would decline by 2.5 percent a year, while the dividend share would correspondingly rise.

After ten years, the Transition Fund would expire and 100 percent of the revenue would be paid out in dividends.

One other feature of the Sky Trust—its so-called safety valve—is designed to ease the impact of higher carbon prices on the U.S. economy. Here's how it works. Assume that in the first year, the trust issues permits for 1.3 billion tons of carbon (the amount the U.S. emitted in 1990). Driven by demand, the market would then set a price for those 1.3 billion permits. The trouble is, no one knows what this price will be, and this uncertainty could reduce investment. So, to allay uncertainty and prevent a price jolt, the Sky Trust includes a first-year price ceiling of $25 a ton. This means that if the market drives the price *above* $25 a ton, the Trust would sell enough additional permits at $25 a ton to keep the price that year from rising higher. Then, for the next four years, the price ceiling would gradually rise.

Now, $25 a ton is not a big deal. It's the equivalent of 6 cents a gallon of gas—far less than gas prices rose in 2000 without any help from carbon emission limits. It would still leave U.S. fuel prices at roughly half the level of Europe and Japan, and would barely be noticed by the American economy. While the price ceiling was in effect, future supply and demand for carbon permits—and hence future prices—would become much clearer. Businesses would have time to adjust to the now more certain economic future, and consumers could think about their next car. Meanwhile, dividends and transition payments would kick in.

Note that the Sky Trust is *not* linked to the Kyoto Protocol. This agreement, signed in 1997, has not been ratified by the U.S. Senate, and may never be. Instead, the Sky Trust's carbon target is based on the Rio Treaty of 1992, signed by President George Bush and ratified unanimously by the Senate. While the Kyoto Protocol would cap U.S. carbon emissions at 7 percent *below* the 1990 level, the Rio Treaty's initial goal *is* the 1990 level. Given that we're now emitting carbon at about 15 percent *above* our 1990 rate, this is a more realistic starting point—and one that's been approved by the Senate.

Back to the Future

It's 2010. You and your kids just received $644 apiece from the U.S. Sky Trust. The money was transferred electronically into your Charles

Schwab accounts. Since Janice and Alan have Individual Development Accounts, their dividends will accumulate tax-free until they are eighteen. You're happy, and as you do every year, you take a spare moment to check the Sky Trust Web site.

"The past year has been an excellent one for the beneficial owners of the Sky Trust," begins a letter from Board of Trustees Chair Elizabeth Dole. "Your trustees are pleased to report that while use of our primary asset, the atmosphere's carbon absorption capacity, declined 4 percent last year, prices rose by over 10 percent. Thus, we earned $184 billion, a $5 billion increase from the previous year. This means your annual dividend is the highest ever. Please use it wisely and well!"

You click to the latest quarterly finanical statements. It's easy to see, thanks to a simple graph, how much money came in and how much went out. Almost all the revenue came from sales of carbon emission permits; there was a little extra from interest. On the outflow side, there was a tiny amount (less than the interest earned) spent on administration, and $23 billion (12.5 percent of revenue) dedicated to the Transition Fund. All the rest ($161 billion) was distributed in equal dividends to U.S. citizens.

A photo of the blue earth from space catches your eye. You click on it and zip to the State of Our Sky page. Here, the trustees report that the carbon dioxide concentration inched upward last year, as did the average global temperature. On the positive side, the ozone hole in the Southern Hemisphere was slightly smaller, and acid rain in the United States was down considerably. The trustees go on to say that the number of permits issued next year will be 3.2 percent below this year's level.

A question pops into your mind: Why 3.2 percent? You think this might be a frequently asked question, so you click the FAQs button and scroll through the Q & A list.

When was the Sky Trust founded?

The U.S. Sky Trust was founded in 2003 when Congress passed the Atmospheric Protection Act by a two-to-one majority.

What is the mission of the U.S. Sky Trust?

The Sky Trust has three purposes: (1) to protect the atmosphere for future generations; (2) to assure that those who use the atmosphere for waste storage pay a market price for doing so; and (3) to divide revenue from the atmosphere equally among all U.S. citizens.

How do I become a U.S. Sky Trust shareholder?

You can register on-line at <www.skytrust.org>, or at any bank, credit union, or savings institution. Only U.S. citizens with a valid Social Security number can register. At the time you register, you must identify a bank or securities account to which dividends can be transfered electronically. If you have no such account, the Sky Trust will retain your dividends until you open one. Parents are responsible for registering and opening accounts for their children up to age eighteen.

How many Sky Trust shares can I get?

Each citizen is entitled to one and only one U.S. Sky Trust share. All shares carry the right to one vote in shareholder elections.

Can I sell my Sky Trust share to someone else?

No. Like your citizenship, your U.S. Sky Trust share belongs to you and you alone. You cannot sell or give it to anyone. When you die, your share dies with you.

How are Sky Trust dividends calculated?

All revenue from carbon emission permit sales is put into a pool. From this pool are subtracted all administrative costs, and all contributions to the Transition Fund (see below). The amount remaining is then divided by the total number of U.S. citizens who have registered to become Sky Trust shareholders. The result is the equal dividend that's sent to all shareholders in December.

Will my Sky Trust dividends go up or down?

There are no guarantees with regard to Sky Trust dividends. Like all dividends, the amount depends on financial results. Since the Sky Trust started, however—especially since price ceilings were lifted in

2009—per capita revenue has trended upward. It is management's expectation that this trend will continue for several more years.

Will my Sky Trust dividends be taxed?

Like all dividends, Sky Trust dividends are subject to income taxation. However, adults over eighteen may place their Sky Trust dividends into qualified Individual Retirement Accounts, in which case the dividends will not be taxed.

Will my children's Sky Trust dividends be taxed?

Children's dividends will be taxed at the parent's tax rate unless they are deposited into a qualified Individual Development Account. In that event, they will be allowed to accumulate tax-free. After the child reaches eighteen, s/he may withdraw from the IDA for education, first home purchase, or a small business in which s/he is a principal, without tax consequences.

What is the Transition Fund?

The Sky Trust Transition Fund was created to assist families and communities whose livelihoods are adversely affected by the shift from carbon-based fuels. Types of transition assistance include unemployment compensation, pension fund contributions, gasoline credits, energy conservation grants, and winter home heating credits if you live in a cold climate zone.

How is the Sky Trust governed?

The U.S. Sky Trust is a not-for-profit shareholder trust incorporated in Massachusetts. It is governed by a nine-person board of trustees, each member of whom has a fiduciary responsibility to all current and future U.S. citizens.

How are trustees chosen?

The first trustees were appointed by the president and confirmed by the U.S. Senate. Their terms were staggered from three to eleven years. As each appointed member's term expires, the vacant seats are filled by shareholder election. The chair is elected by the trustees from among board members.

Who decides how many carbon storage permits to sell?

Each year the board of trustees decides, by majority vote, how many carbon emission permits to sell. By law, the trustees must take into account the following factors:

- the measures taken by other countries
- the physiochemical state of the atmosphere
- economic and regional impacts

Well, you think, the U.S. economy is strong, the European Union is rapidly cutting its carbon emissions, and China has agreed not to build more coal-fired power plants—that might explain the 3.2 percent cut in next year's emissions. In any case, you feel good. You like knowing a little more about the planet, and what it takes to keep the planet fit for life. You like having a *stake* in preserving the planet for Janice and Alan. You're happy you're not being ripped off. And yes, you appreciate the dividends. Now what was the name, you suddenly wonder, of that politician who set this thing up?

What Will You Do with Your Dividends?

The nice thing about predictable dividends is that you can plan what to do with them. People in Alaska do this every year. The sums involved aren't trivial, especially for large families. And the possibilities are many.

In 1995, the Permanent Fund surveyed Alaskans to see how they actually used their dividends. It found that the largest number used their dividends to pay bills, but a substanial number saved them for education and rainy days.

With Sky Trust dividends, you and your children would have similar choices every year. In addition, you could have a tax incentive to save your dividend rather than spend it. Thus, if you put your dividend into an Individual Retirement Account, you'd pay no immediate taxes, and

WHAT ALASKANS DO WITH THEIR DIVIDENDS

- 33% spend it all
- 25% save it all
- 42% spend some and save some
- Top savings goals:
    Education (30%)
    "Rainy day" (24%)
    Retirement (20%)
- Top spending uses:
    Bills (45%)
    Medical expenses (10%)
    Travel (10%)

Figure 8
Source: Alaska Permanent Fund, 1995 Survey <www.apfc.org>.

your earnings could grow tax-free. And you could put your kids' dividends into tax-free Individual Development Accounts, as Jay Hammond once envisioned.

Of course, you might use part of your dividend to pay higher utility bills. But if you've conserved, or cut back on other expenses, you might not have to. Then you could take your dividend and save it for something special. Or you could boost that retirement account your financial adviser said was too small. And your kids could stash money away for college.

I don't want to exaggerate. The Sky Trust won't make you a millionaire. You'll still have to work for a living. Though your kids will be trust fund babies, their inheritances won't rival the Rockefellers'. But who's to say what the future holds? Rome wasn't built in a day. When Ida May Fuller received the first Social Security check in 1940, it was for $22.50; now the average monthly benefit exceeds $800. As the twenty-first century progresses, gifts of nature besides the sky will become scarce and therefore valuable. The Sky Trust would establish the principle that scarcity rent from commonly inherited assets belongs to all of us. Like the original Social Security Act, it would lay pipes through which more money could later flow. Perhaps a portfolio of dividend-paying trusts might one day be a birthright of Americans, extending the notion of one person, one vote, to one person, one *share*. The implications of *that* would be far-reaching.

Viewed in this way, the establishment of a U.S. Sky Trust would be an historic event, comparable to the Homestead Act of 1862, the Federal Reserve Act of 1913, and the Social Security Act of 1935. Like the Homestead Act, a Sky Trust would create a new class of property owners—in effect, every citizen would have an equity stake in the sky. Beyond this, the Sky Trust would establish an independent board of trustees to manage the carbon flow through our economy, much as the Fed manages the money flow. And, like the Social Security Act, it would define a new algorithm for moving money within our economy: *from* all according to their use of a commons, *to* all according to their equal ownership.

The importance of this new algorithm can't be overstated. It differs significantly from the algorithms of both Social Security and public assistance. The underlying formula for public assistance is, *from* all according to their tax liability, *to* all according to their need. The underlying formula for Social Security is, *from* all according to their wages, *to* all according to their longevity and disability. Both these algorithms, though broadly accepted, are not without controversy. More important, they've gone about as far as they can go—public assistance because Americans don't like taxing Peter to pay Paul, and Social Security because payroll taxes can't get much higher.

The new Sky Trust algorithm, by contrast, has room to grow. It channels money from overusers of nature to underusers, and as nature gets scarcer, more money can flow this way. Moreover, it's hard to argue against the Sky Trust's algorithm. That consumers should pay for what they use is among the oldest principles of markets; here it's simply extended to an asset we had foolishly priced at zero. Similarly, that dividends should flow to property owners is a sacred tenet of capitalism. The only novelty here is that of equal and universal ownership of a commons.

But how else could ownership of the sky be divided? Most people accept the notion that human-made assets should be unequally distributed in order to encourage individual effort. But how can you argue that sky ownership should be unequally divided? After all, no person lifted a finger to create it. The atmosphere is a purely inherited asset, and not from anyone's parents, but from the common creation.

A U.S. Sky Trust, in sum, would marry the cap-and-trade system for rationing a scarce gift of nature with a trust for preserving common ownership. It would thereby remedy not only the ecological tragedy of the commons, but also the oft-forgotten loss of the commons by the commoners. And it would do both jobs without sacrificing freedom.

That, ultimately, is the elegance of this new product. It's equitable, ecological, *and* market-based. It avoids taxes and government bureaucracy. And it's very customer friendly. Is there any other mechanism that could better help us adapt to the scarcity of sky? If there is, I've yet to see it.

On Pain

There are, of course, those who say that *any* policy that limits the amount of carbon we burn will cause great harm to the American people. Our Gross Domestic Product will shrink, consumers will be poorer, and hundreds of thousands of workers will lose jobs. "All pain, no gain" was for a time the mantra of these Cassandras. And to "prove" their point, they'd cite numbers from computer models of the U.S. economy.

So let me say a word about computer models. Having written a few business plans, I know what can be done with numbers, especially when they're *predictive* rather than *descriptive*. Not to put too fine a point on it, numbers can predict almost anything you want them to. Assumptions can be changed, formulas can be tweaked, and *voilà*, your bias is confirmed. For every computer run that forecasts two-hundred thousand jobs lost, I can get you another that predicts three-hundred thousand jobs gained.

What *is* undeniable, though, is that change causes pain. It's always hard to adapt to the new, often harder to let go of the old. Whenever a new industry emerges, or an old one dies, some people gain and others lose.

Since change is inevitable, and always causes pain to someone, it makes sense for societies to develop rules about pain sharing. We'd expect these rules to reflect the tension between our desire for change and our fear of it, to seesaw between coldheartedness and compassion. And they do. Thus, when workers are unemployed, we pay part, but not all, of their lost salaries. When businesses go bankrupt, we protect some, but not all, of their creditors. When there's a hurricane or other natural disaster, we rush government and private aid to victims, while knowing there's no compensation for the death of loved ones.

Inevitably, the rules on pain sharing are inelegant, and injustices occur. Why were workers who lost their jobs for one reason given compensation, while others who lost their jobs for different reasons given nothing? Why were one company's stockholders bailed out by taxpayers, while others weren't? The answers to such questions are inevitably political: because this group of workers had a strong union, because that company's CEO had connections. And there always are, at the end of the day, real losers.

All this is by way of saying that climate change, like all change, will cause pain. At the extreme, it will cause a large number of people to lose their homes, health, and livelihoods. At a minimum, it will cause a smaller number of people to lose jobs and money. The politics of climate change is thus, to a great degree, the politics of pain management. The Sky Trust doesn't deny this. On the contrary, it consciously seeks to minimize the pain from climate change, and to share what pain there is as equitably as possible.

Over the long run, the key to minimizing pain is to minimize the geophysical effects of climate change—rising sea levels, extreme weather, the spread of tropical diseases to now temperate zones. That can be accomplished by cutting carbon burning as quickly as possible. The short-run task is different: it is to lessen the economic pain of reduced carbon burning. The Sky Trust approaches this task in three ways.

First is its reliance on gradualism. Given time and forewarning, the U.S. economy is amazingly resilient. What caused gas lines in the 1970s was a large, *sudden* jump in oil prices. The five-year phase-in of the Sky Trust is designed to avert this. During this period, carbon prices would start low and rise gradually. This would add a few nickels per gallon to the price of gasoline, and a few pennies per kilowatt to the price of electricity—increases that could easily be offset by minor efficiency improvements or lifestyle changes. Everyone would know in advance what prices were coming. Investments in conservation, new energy technologies, and fuel-efficient automobiles could be planned accordingly.

The Sky Trust's second pain-reducing tool is its use of scarcity rent to pay dividends. Absent some way to offset higher carbon burning prices, all Americans would lose buying power. With dividends, most Americans' buying power would be protected. In fact, because of the dividends, many Americans would come out ahead—even without taking steps to conserve. By conserving they could gain even more. And most of those who don't conserve—that is, those who consciously or lazily fail to pursue cost reductions—would be able to afford their higher costs.

The Sky Trust's third pain reducer is its Transition Fund. To the extent that anyone can be fairly compensated for losing his or her livelihood, the Transition Fund could do it. A rough estimate is that it would have up to $25 billion a year to spend for ten years—enough to pay more than we've ever paid to workers displaced for any reason.

Of course, not all the transition money would go to laid-off workers. Some would go to low-income consumers, some to hard-hit communities. These choices would be made by Congress, the states, and local governments. The point is that, thanks to its capture of scarcity rent, the Sky Trust would have enough money to make these pain reductions possible.

And what about the economy as a whole? Nowadays, those who prescribe medicine for the American economy must take a kind of Hippocratic oath; they must be extremely confident their cure won't be worse than the disease. I'm quite confident this is so for the Sky Trust—that the pain from a Sky Trust would be nothing compared to the pain that would result from global warming. Why do I think this? Mainly because our economy is already full of scarcities with prices well above zero. The freeness of air, far from being typical, is an anomaly. Pricing sky the way we price everything else won't be a very big deal, especially if we do it gradually. On the other hand, the costs of *not* curbing climate change are likely to be quite high.

My confidence also comes from looking around the world. Other industrial nations—who pay much more for gas than we do—have shown it's possible to extract more benefit from a unit of carbon than we do. What these countries tell us is that there's a lot of carbon fat in the U.S. economy. We can lose some of that flab and still be healthy and strong.

In fact, we've already started to do this. According to the U.S. Energy Information Agency, U.S. oil expenditures have fallen from 8.5 percent of GDP in 1981 to 3 percent in 1999. Even energy-intensive industries like the airlines have been on a fossil fuel diet. In 1981, jet fuel accounted for 30 percent of airline operating expenses, according to the Air Transport Association. Now, thanks to more efficient planes, fuel represents just 10 percent of operating costs.

Then there are the computer runs. As I said earlier, computer runs can "prove" almost anything. Still, they can be useful for alerting us to potentially serious swings in one direction or another. Seen in this light, the growing number of carbon-related econometric studies offers reassurance. Some predict a small, brief slowing in GDP *growth* (not in GDP itself) due to higher carbon prices. None predicts a large or a long slowing. One predicts a small positive impact as higher carbon prices spur innovation and new investment. (For details, see the Barrett, Charles River Associates, Energy Information Administration, Interlaboratory Working Group, Probyn, Repetto, Tellus Institute, WEFA, and Weyant works cited in the bibliography.)

What exactly does this mean? It means, above all, that the Sky Trust won't cause an economic recession. Even in the worst case scenarios, GDP *doesn't fall*—it simply grows slower (in the computer's mind) than it would grow (in the same computer's mind) with lower carbon prices. In other words, there'll be more jobs and more wealth no matter what happens to carbon prices—the only question is how much more. The recycling of scarcity rent is a key reason for this—it assures that consumer buying power is maintained.

Beyond this, it's impossible to draw conclusions. Since a multitude of variables affect our economy, singling out one tells us little about what the future holds. Further, GDP itself may be a misleading guide. If global warming causes more extreme weather events, the damage inflicted could actually *increase* GDP by boosting spending on reconstruction. Conversely, a decrease in carbon emissions would have side benefits (such as fewer cases of asthma and other pollution-caused diseases) which, just as ironically, would cause a *decrease* in health care spending, and thus of GDP. The bottom line is that while we can't predict the future with great precision, we *can* design a system that minimizes people's pain, and even gives many of them a gain. That's exactly what the Sky Trust would do.

If I had to bet my own money on the macroeconomic effects of a Sky Trust, I'd be bullish. I'd bet a Sky Trust makes our economy stronger rather than weaker. Yes, the scarcity of sky will show up as a new cost of goods sold. But far from being a barrier to growth, I see that as a spur. I think the American economy works best when it rises to meet challenges.

I can't prove this. I *can* cite a statement signed by twenty-five hundred economists, including eight Nobel laureates, that says: "Sound economic analysis shows that there are policy options that would slow climate change without harming American living standards, and these measures may in fact improve U.S. productivity in the long run." The Sky Trust—though not specifically endorsed by the economists—is one such policy option.

And I have other evidence. Twenty years ago, utilities projected large increases in the amount of electricity America would "demand," and hence of the fuel they'd need to burn. A physicist named Amory Lovins disagreed. Lovins said our economy could do just fine with *less* fuel rather than more. Further, Lovins argued, utilities themselves could earn more money by selling less energy. Less could truly be more. Fewer units sold could yield more growth and more profit—if the rate structure was right.

With nudging from environmentalists and state regulatory commissions, utilities tried out Lovins' ideas. They built fewer power plants and invested in conservation instead. As Lovins predicted, they wound up with lower cost structures and higher profits. And the U.S. economy boomed.

If electric utilities—who are *in the business* of burning carbon—can make more money by burning less carbon, surely other businesses can do so, too. What's required is a combination of incentives and ingenuity. The Sky Trust provides the former; American management and workers will provide the latter.

Who doubts that we'll continue to adapt and grow? There'll be less carbon burning and more e-mailing, less of an economy of things and more of an economy of mind. There'll be growth of a different color, but growth nonetheless. The Sky Trust, at the very least, won't stop this growth. I think it will spur it.

ADAM SMITH
1723–1790
Scottish philosopher and economist

"As soon as the land of any country has all become private property, the landlords, like all other men, love to reap where they never sowed, and demand a rent even for its natural produce."
—*The Wealth of Nations,* 1776

JAMES WATT
1736–1819
Scottish inventor

His steam engine ushered in the era of fossil fuel burning. He also invented a governor to keep the steam engine from going too fast.

JAMES MADISON
1751–1836
*Father of the Bill of Rights and
fourth President of the United States*

"The powers not delegated to the United States by the Constitution,
nor prohibited by it to the States, are reserved to the States respectively,
or to the people."
—Ninth Amendment to the U.S. Constitution

JOHN MCADAM
1756–1836
Scottish engineer

He invented a technique of road paving using crushed stones and asphalt. Millions
of miles of paved roads now disturb and fragment habitats worldwide.

DAVID RICARDO
1772–1823
English stockbroker and economist

"[If] air, water, the elasticity of steam, and the pressure of the atmosphere, were of various qualities; if they could be appropriated, and each quality existed only in moderate abundance, they, as well as the land, would afford a rent, as the successive qualities were brought into use."

—*On The Principles of Political Economy and Taxation,* 1817

By Courtesy of the National Portrait Gallery, London

SAMUEL PLIMSOLL
1824–1898
Member of Parliament

He led the campaign for load lines on merchant ships.

By Courtesy of the National Portrait Gallery, London

SVANTE ARRHENIUS
1859–1927
Swedish chemist and
Nobel Prize winner

"A simple calculation shows that the temperature in the arctic regions would rise about 8° to 9°C, if the carbonic acid [carbon dioxide] increased to 2.5 or 3 times its present value."

—*On the Influence of Carbonic Acid in the Air upon the Temperature of the Ground,* 1896

© Hulton-Deutsch/CORBIS

HENRY FORD
1863–1947
American industrialist

"I will build a motor car for the great multitude . . . so low in price that no man making a good salary will be unable to own one and enjoy with his family the blessing of hours of pleasure in God's great open spaces."

© Bettman/CORBIS

GUGLIELMO MARCONI
1874–1937
Italian scientist, businessman,
and Nobel Prize winner

His invention of wireless radio turned the electromagnetic spectrum into an extremely valuable asset.

© Bettman/CORBIS

ARTHUR PIGOU
1877–1959
English economist

"It is possible for the state, if it so chooses, to remove the divergence [between internal and external costs] . . . with bounties [i.e., subsidies] and taxes."

—*The Economics of Welfare*, 1920

Courtesy of Mark Blaug

JOHN MAYNARD KEYNES
1883–1946
English economist

"A point may soon be reached, much sooner perhaps than we are all of us aware of, when [essential] needs are satisfied . . . [and] we prefer to devote our further energies to non-economic purposes."
—*Economic Possibilities for our Grandchildren,* 1930

© Bettman/CORBIS

THOMAS MIDGELY JR.
1889–1944
American industrial chemist

Working for General Motors, he invented leaded gasoline and chlorofluorocarbons (CFCs). Both seemed safe at first but, when massively used, proved dangerous to human health and the ozone layer.

Courtesy of the American Chemical Society

KENNETH BOULDING
1910–1993
American economist

"The atmosphere may become man's major problem in another generation, at the rate at which we are filling it up with gunk."
—*The Economics of the Coming Spaceship Earth*, 1966

RONALD COASE
1910–
*English-American economist
and Nobel Prize winner*

"The proposal to solve the smoke-pollution and similar problems by the
use of taxes bristles with difficulties."
—*The Problem of Social Cost*, 1960

GARRETT HARDIN
1915–
American biologist

"The rational man finds that his share of the cost of the wastes he discharges into the commons is less than the cost of purifying his wastes before releasing them. Since this is true for everyone, we are locked into a system of 'fouling our own nest.'"

—*The Tragedy of the Commons,* 1968

JAY HAMMOND
1922–
Republican governor of
Alaska, 1972–1980

He founded the Alaska Permanent Fund, which shares Alaska's oil wealth equally among its citizens.

JULIAN SIMON
1932–1998
American economist

"More people, and increased income, cause resources to become more scarce in the short run. Heightened scarcity causes prices to rise. The higher prices present opportunity, and prompt inventors and entrepreneurs to search for solutions."

—*The Ultimate Resource,* 1998

Courtesy of Rita Simon

Chapter 6

Thought Experiments for Economists

The ideas of economists and political philosophers, both
when they are right and when they are wrong, are more
powerful than is commonly understood. Indeed, the
world is ruled by little else.
—John Maynard Keynes

Imagination is more important than knowledge.
—Albert Einstein

1991
United States wins Gulf War; Bush soars in polls.
Carbon dioxide concentration in the air: 355 parts per million
Average temperature at surface of the earth: 58.0°F

W hen I began writing this book, the question "Who owns the
sky?" was like a Zen koan—a seemingly innocent query that,
upon reflection, opens many unexpected doors. What I discovered was
that this line of inquiry is particularly fertile. Thus, if you accept the
notion that the sky belongs to all of us, you soon wonder if there's a
practical way to structure common ownership. (Answer: yes.) Like-

wise, if you start with the premise that the sky is a valuable asset that shouldn't be given away free, you soon pose the question, "Are there other assets like this?" (Answer: yes.) You then ask whether there's a whole *class* of hidden assets—like the dark matter of the universe—that should be better priced and owned by all of us. And you go on to inquire, "If this were so, what difference would it make?"

Such musings have occupied me for the past several years. They've also led me to ponder why so few economists engage in thought experiments of this type. As far as I can tell, the majority of economists are content to accept, if not sanctify, the prevailing conventions. They rarely shift to what Buddhists call "beginner's mind." But we can. So please, even if you're not an economist or a Buddhist, read on. I'll explain what's wrong with prevailing economic thinking. And I'll offer four thought experiments to exemplify how, in my view, twenty-first-century economists *ought* to think.

What If?

Among the root assumptions of conventional economics are (1) there are no limits imposed by nature, (2) "externalities" such as pollution are minor and inconsequential, and (3) more stuff equals more happiness. These premises are wrong and dangerous. The truth—or at least a better starting point—is that nature is now the scarcest economic factor, externalities are now large and consequential, and happiness is now only partially a function of stuff. If you substitute these latter assumptions for the former, lots of things change.

Note the word "now" in the preceding paragraph. I grant that, in days gone by, the conventional assumptions better approximated reality. A hundred years ago, in the heyday of classical economics, nature *did* seem infinite, externalities *did* appear inconsequential, and more stuff *did* create more happiness. But times change and so should economists. Our once spacious skies are no longer so. The externalized costs of pesticides, toxic wastes, water and air pollution, clear-cut forests, and loss of biodiversity, are today too large to be ignored. And a kind of threshold has been reached in rich countries beyond which the accumulation of more stuff adds little, if any, happiness to the well-off. Yet, in the face of these obvious changes, economists cling to the delusion that their old assumptions continue to work. As John Kenneth Galbraith has remarked, "the shortcomings of economics are not original error but uncorrected obsolescence."

Another assumption at the core of economics is "A rising tide lifts all boats"—that is, growth benefits everyone. We all know this isn't necessarily so. When economic tides rise today, all *yachts* rise with them, but many small boats don't. Thus, according to the Federal Reserve, only the top 5 percent of U.S. households saw an increase in their net worth from 1983 to 1997; wealth declined for everyone else. Moreover, according to Edward N. Wolff, the financial wealth of the top 5 percent of American households now exceeds the *combined* financial wealth of the bottom 95 percent—as extreme an imbalance as is found in the poorest countries of the world.

Most economists accept these statistics but ignore their meaning—that our market system as it exists today isn't "plumbed" to allocate wealth equitably. Whether tides rise or fall, the pipes through which money flows to a small number of Americans are much thicker than the pipes through which money flows to everyone else. This is due to our laws of property and inheritance. But most economists, while they lament the *effects* of bad plumbing, show little interest in remedying the *causes*.

With this background, I offer four thought experiments. All begin with root assumptions that, in my view, reflect today's reality more accurately than does prevailing economic thinking. All then follow those assumptions to logical and practical "upgrades" in property laws or market rules. Though this may seem like an exercise in whimsy, it's akin to the scientific method—pose a hypothesis and then test it—as well as to modern business methods—ask "what if?" and plug different scenarios into a computer. It's what people do when searching for new theories or new products.

1. Imagine waste sinks are scarce.

I trust by now you agree we're running out of sky. Let's assume other industrial waste sinks—land, water, our own bodies—can also safely absorb only so much. What then?

Economists' standard model of the human economy looks like this:

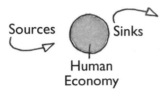

Figure 9. Standard Model: Unlimited Sinks

This standard model assumes an ever-growing human economy will always have enough sources and sinks to thrive in. In this pre-Copernican view of the world, the human economy sits—and will *always* sit—at the center of an infinite universe of possibility.

Ecological economists like Herman Daly contend this model is outdated. These economists are today a small minority of the profession, but like Copernicus five hundred years ago, they're on to something. They make two small but important changes in the above diagram. First, they draw a circle around it, and second, they picture the human economy as expanding into the larger circle. Thus:

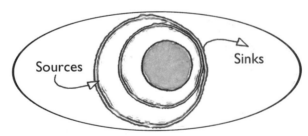

Figure 10. Real World: Sinks Limited by Nature

Adding the outer circle makes the human economy a subsystem of a larger system, which you can call nature, the natural economy, the biosphere or Gaia, according to your taste. This larger system, like every system, has a boundary. Within this boundary, molecules move around continuously, but rarely escape. Hydrogen and oxygen, bound together as water, cycle from ocean to sky to river to ocean, transporting other molecules along the way. Nitrogen cycles from air to soil to plants to animals to air. Carbon and a myriad of other compounds cycle similarly. Energy from the sun drives the whole system, and gravity holds it together. Somehow, this larger system has run nonstop for three and a half billion years, allowing life to flourish.

Placing the human economy inside this larger system brings into play the elements of *scale* and *time*—scale because the size of the human economy relative to the larger economy now matters, and time because that relative size changes over the years. Thus, on the time axis, the human economy appears literally in the fifty-ninth minute of the eleventh hour of the natural economy's history, and for most of its brief life is so small it's barely noticed by nature. But then something momentous happens—something crudely comparable to the Big Bang. About a hundred years ago—in roughly the last second of the last minute of nature's long history—the human economy explodes. Suddenly, like a balloon stuffing itself with air, this once static inner circle bursts out toward the edges of the larger circle.

This change in scale over time causes more trouble than you might think. In the old days, the human economy's mission was simple: to grow as fast as possible. Today, with the boundaries of nature fast approaching, that mission is more complicated: to increase our contentment without destroying our nest. Rules that encourage fast growth aren't likely to be the same as those that protect our nest or add contentment. Some new rules may be necessary.

Daly tells a revealing story about these diagrams. In 1992, the World Bank (where Daly worked) was preparing a report called *Development and the Environment.* An early draft contained a drawing entitled "The Relationship Between the Economy and the Environment," which looked much like our diagram of the standard model. It had a square labeled "Economy," an arrow coming in labeled "Inputs" and an arrow going out labeled "Outputs"—and nothing more. Daly suggested it would be a good idea to draw a larger box around the one depicted, in order to represent the "Environment."

The next draft included the same diagram with an unlabeled box around it like a picture frame. Daly commented that the larger box ought to be *labeled* "Environment," or else it was merely decorative. The final draft omitted the diagram altogether.

A few months later, the chief economist of the World Bank, Larry Summers, was on a panel discussing the book *Beyond the Limits*, which includes a diagram like the one Daly proposed. Daly was in the audience, and asked Summers if, looking at that diagram, he thought the question of the size of human economy relative to the natural economy was important. Summers's reply was brusque: "That's not the right way to look at it." Summers then went on to serve as President Clinton's Secretary of the Treasury.

Economic Jujitsu

Let's now, in our thought experiment, assume the existence of a natural economy in which sinks, if not sources, are limited. Let's then ask the question: What's the best way to let the human economy grow—and at the same time, keep it from filling nature's sinks? Let's posit that any solution should be compatible with the basic tenets of capitalism—after all, we want an upgrade, not a new operating system. What new rules or laws might we devise?

Ideally, what we'd want is a mechanism like the governor in a steam engine—a device that automatically slows a system when it runs too fast or too hot. Thus, as a steam engine gets hotter, a spindle spins faster and centrifugal force lifts two flyballs on hinged arms. This movement decreases the size of the steam inlet valve, slowing the engine.

An analogous governor for the human economy might work like this. As the economy fills the sky with carbon, market forces lift the price of the sky's remaining carbon storage capacity. Demand for carbon then falls, reducing the amount of carbon entering the economy. In this case, the magic of scarcity rent replaces the lifting power of centrifugal force.

What's the point here? Right now, with regard to sinks, the global economy is dominated by perverse feedback loops—that is, waste dumping breeds more waste dumping. Advanced countries get rich by filling up sinks; less advanced countries then try to catch up. This works if sinks

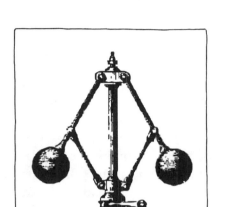

Figure 11. Steam Engine Governor
The steam engine governor is a device that automatically slows the engine down when it runs too fast or too hot.

are infinite, but not if sinks are scarce. If sinks are scarce, these perverse feedback loops must be replaced, jujitsu-like, by virtuous ones. When nature's thresholds are approached, less needs to become more; the gains from *not* polluting need to become greater than the gains from polluting. Fortunately, there are mechanisms like the Sky Trust that can do this. The task before us is to design and install them.

2. *Imagine externalities are large.*

An economist's definition of an "externality" is a cost that markets *don't* recognize. For example, when a factory emits pollution, causing people downwind to get sick, the victims' pain and medical bills aren't part of the polluter's costs. Similarly, when jet noise near an airport lowers property values, neither the engine makers nor the airlines pick up the tab.

For a long time, economists believed externalities were trivial. In any case, the tools developed by economists to measure economic activity—most notably, the Gross Domestic Product—either ignore the existence of externalities, or worse yet, count them as *positive contributions*. Thus, when Exxon spends billions of dollars to remedy the damages from an oil

Accounting

spill, those expenditures *add* to the Gross Domestic Product, despite the fact that the spill's damages are nowhere counted as losses. As Jonathan Rowe has written,

> By the curious standard of the GDP, the nation's economic hero is a terminal cancer patient who is going through a costly divorce. The happiest event is an earthquake or a hurricane. The most desirable habitat is a multibillion-dollar Superfund site. All these add to the GDP, because they cause money to change hands. It is as if a business kept a balance sheet by merely adding up all transactions, without distinguishing between income and expenses.

The world *illth* isn't one economists frequently employ. It was coined in the nineteenth century by art critic and economist John Ruskin, who saw in Dickens's England how factories created not only wealth but squalor. Ruskin defined *illth* as acts "causing various devastation and trouble." It strikes me as a handy term, yet it's disappeared from every dictionary and economics text I've checked. I'd like to revive it.

It's not surprising illth occurs. In life, there are always trade-offs. A three-scoop chocolate sundae may taste great, but your waistline and arteries pay a price. Drugs have side effects, industrial processes generate waste, and military actions cause collateral damage. Ordinary double-entry bookkeeping recognizes this. Everyone's income is someone else's expense; every asset has an offsetting liability. Yet for some reason, economist pay little attention to the darker side of the economic ledger.

Illth has grown enormously since the nineteenth century. When horses were the primary mode of transport, the illth they produced—manure—was smelly but not terribly dangerous. Today, the illth from cars isn't only smelly, it also threatens to melt polar ice caps. What's more, the speed at which all cars move (at least in many U.S. cities) is falling as more cars are added. Congestion, not mobility, is rising.

A rough estimate of current illth has been made by my former colleagues at Redefining Progress, and it's staggering. RP measured sixteen kinds of illth in America and found they cost $4.4 trillion in 1998. By contrast, the official GDP that year was $7.6 trillion, a good chunk of which was illth disguised as wealth. In other words, *our combined hustling and bustling in 1998 may have done more harm than good.* We think we got richer, while in fact our well-being diminished.

While these numbers are certainly crude, they inspire a follow-up query: For how long has illth been this large? Again, Redefining Progress sheds some light. It calculated something called the Genuine Progress Indicator (GPI) for every year dating back to 1950. The GPI is a derivative of GDP. It *adds* many things GDP leaves out—such as the value of unpaid household labor and volunteer work—and *subtracts* the illth costs listed above. Redefining Progress found that, from 1950 to 1972, the GDP and GPI both trended upward. Then, in the early 1970s, the two

	($ billion)
Cost of household pollution abatement	12
Cost of noise pollution	16
Cost of crime	28
Cost of air pollution	38
Cost of water pollution	50
Cost of family breakdown	59
Loss of old-growth forests	83
Cost of underemployment	112
Cost of automobile accidents	126
Loss of farmland	130
Loss of leisure time	276
Cost of ozone depletion	306
Loss of wetlands	363
Cost of commuting	386
Cost of long-term environmental damage	1,054
Depletion of nonrenewable resources	1,333
TOTAL: $4.372 trillion	

Figure 12. Costs of Illth in the United States, 1998
Source: Why Bigger Isn't Better: The Genuine Progress Indicator Update, Redefining Progress, November 1999.

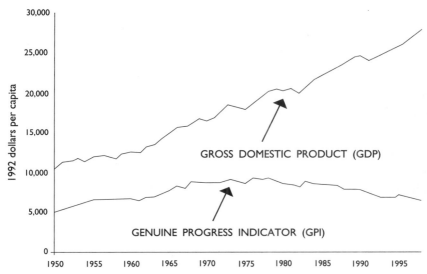

Figure 13. U.S. Gross Domestic Product vs. Genuine Progress Indicator, 1950 to 1998

This graph shows the divergence in the early 1970s between Gross Domestic Product—the sum of all monetary transactions—and a measure of well-being called the Genuine Progress Indicator. The graph suggests that the increase in illth created by U.S. economic activity now exceeds the gain in well-being.

Source: Redefining Progress.

measurements diverged—GDP kept rising, while GPI began to fall. This divergence has continued ever since.

Though the composition of the GPI is somewhat arbitrary, the implications of this finding are far-reaching. They suggest that roughly twenty-five years ago, a turning point was reached. On the far side of this turning point, where we are today, the rate at which our economy creates illth quite possibly *exceeds* the rate at which it creates wealth. In economic lingo, we may have reached a point of *negative marginal return.*

This shouldn't be surprising. The world is full of declining marginal utilities, and economists are well aware of the phenomenon. To a hungry person, one steak has high marginal utility, a second steak has less marginal utility, and a third steak probably has none. Indeed, if the person eats the third steak and gets sick, it would have *negative* marginal utility.

What if our entire economy consumes the equivalent of three steaks? It's at least plausible that additional food might cause more harm than good.

What *is* surprising is this: If the marginal return on economic activity has been declining for a quarter of a century—forget about being *negative*—you'd think economists would take note. You'd think they'd wonder if some of their old assumptions no longer apply. But there's been nary a peep about this from the profession.

The Cost of Goods Sold

It's fun, of course, to criticize economists. But economists aren't the real problem. After all, they're just *measurers* of market activity, not market activity itself. As anthropologist and epistemologist Gregory Bateson was fond of saying, *the map is not the territory*—our picture of reality isn't reality itself. Though economists and their metrics may *blind* us to declining marginal returns, the *causes* of those lowered returns lie elsewhere. They lie, first of all, in the flow of money: A marginal dollar flowing to a rich person adds less happiness than the same dollar flowing to a poor person. And they lie in what's excluded from the cost of goods sold.

What *is* the cost of goods sold? As my City College business instructor explained, "It's everything that goes into your product except overhead and profit." Seems pretty simple. What's not simple, though, is exactly what's included in such broad categories as labor and materials. For example, a company pays for cloth and steel and gasoline, but do its prices include the damage done to forests, watersheds, and airsheds? Another company pays to move a factory from one city to another, but do its costs include the losses to workers and businesses in the abandoned community?

These aren't just accounting questions. They're profound philosophical questions every society must address. When you buy a product, should you or should you not pay, as part of its price, the pro-rated cost of health care for the workers who made it? The cost of disposing the wastes involved in making it—or the wastes that will arise when you're done using it? If not, will these costs be paid by someone else? If so, who and how? If you want to know a people's truest values, pay no attention to what they say. Pay attention to their cost of goods sold. It's there you'll find their collective sense of what really matters and doesn't matter.

There's a lot already included in America's cost of goods sold. For example, Social Security. The deal in our country is, workers and employers each pay half the cost of supporting former workers who are now retired from the labor force. Younger workers accept the deal because they know, or hope, that *they'll* be former workers some day. Employers accept the deal because they can pass the cost on to customers. In other words, Americans support retired people in two ways: partly out of wages, and partly out of what we pay for almost everything we buy. Why is this so? Because as a society, we made a conscious decision to support retired people this way.

Also included in our cost of goods sold is a sum of money reflecting the scarcity of land—it's a portion of what appears on expense statements as "rent." But there's nothing in the cost of things sold that reflects the scarcity of sky. Why not? Because as a society, we've created property rights for land, but not yet for sky.

Here I must express a personal bias. As a rule, I'm a pay-as-you-go kind of guy. Yes, I have two mortgages, but they're fully amortized, so in a sense I'm paying as I go. And yes, I have a few credit cards, but I pay them off every month. Really. My bias is that we *as a society* should also pay as we go to the greatest extent possible. This doesn't mean we should never borrow. Borrowing is justifiable if it leads to an increase in future wealth. What it *does* mean is that we shouldn't squander inherited assets—indeed, we should leave our children *more* than our parents left us. If this truly were our credo, we wouldn't externalize costs. We would, whenever possible, pay them as we go.

As noted earlier, much of what's included in the cost of goods sold is a result of societal choices. Before 1935, nothing was included in the cost of goods sold for workers' retirements. Since 1935, steadily increasing amounts have been included—not only for Social Security, but also for private pensions. The same is true for health care and vacation costs, as well as for many safety and environmental costs. Similarly, the cost of road-building, via excise taxes, is included in the price of gas.

But there's also a lot left out of our cost of goods sold. There's the cost of sky and other scarce ecosystems. There's the cost of defending the Persian Gulf, insuring against nuclear catastrophe, treating environmentally caused illness, and much more. Some of these costs will eventually be paid by taxpayers, some by innocent victims. Some may not be paid for decades, but sooner or later the bills will come due.

Let me be clear about illth. Illth will never go away. It's inherent in our universe. But the *rate* of illth creation can be slowed. More human activity can be conducted in accordance with the Hippocratic oath—first, do no harm. Plimsoll lines can be drawn; prices can be charged. Once illth creation is no longer free, humans *will* create less of it. That's the way things work, or could work. Over time, our rate of illth creation could again be lower than our rate of wealth creation. The marginal return on economic activity could again head upward.

Paying As We Go

The preceding discussion leaves a hanging question. Assuming we *do* want to pay as we go for externalities, how might we actually do that? As an early practitioner of socially responsible business, I first confronted this question in the 1970s. One answer I offered then, as a spokesperson for the California solar industry, was "Give tax credits to solar customers." But this was never a satisfactory answer. It had the virtue of leveling the playing field on which various forms of energy competed, but it didn't pay the external costs of fossil fuel or uranium burning. It equalized *subsidies* rather than costs. Eight years later, when Congress tired of subsidizing clean energy, the prices of solar energy skyrocketed, while the prices of fossil fuels and nuclear power remained right where they'd always been—well below their real costs.

I didn't say it then—I didn't even *think* it then—but it would have been better had Congress created property rights for the sky. That would have *lowered* energy subsidies, not increased them, while leveling competition between clean and unclean energy.

At Working Assets, I approached "paying as we go" in a different way. I asked what we, as a private business, could do to include more social and environmental costs in our own cost of goods sold. Obviously, we were constrained by the market; we couldn't add *too* many costs or we'd be uncompetitive and die. At the same time, being business people, we figured we could derive some benefits—such as lower marketing costs, greater customer loyalty, and better employee morale—by paying some external costs voluntarily. We viewed this as a challenge—to give back to the world while making a profit. And we succeeded.

My Working Assets answer to the question "How can we pay more as we go?" was more satisfying than my solar answer. Still, I wasn't happy. I recognized that in the grand scheme of things, voluntary efforts such as ours could only make a tiny difference. We'd created an interesting model, but not a systemic solution. A systemic solution has to be like Social Security or land rent—a cost all businesses must incur. It can't rest on voluntarism or generosity. If your competitors don't pay for health care or sky, and you choose to do so, your odds of surviving are reduced. To really tackle external costs, *all* firms must pay as they go. There can be no "free riders."

What, then, can be done? That is our thought experiment. Re-enter Arthur Pigou and Ronald Coase. We met these fellows three chapters ago. Pigou's idea was that government should compute externalities and collect them via excise taxes. Coase's idea was that government should create new property rights. Which is the better way to go?

In Pigou's world, politics determine prices, and prices determine the amount of externalities—an indirect and cumbersome process. If you trust politics, this may be fine. But if you think politicians already have enough to do, or that markets are faster and better than politicians at setting prices, then you may favor Coase's approach.

Of course, in Coase's world, politicians aren't out of the picture entirely. They still draw boundaries and assign property rights. But once boundaries are drawn and property rights are assigned, markets pretty much run themselves . Then what we have (assuming transaction costs are low, as they are with a Sky Trust) are nice, self-regulating illth reducers.

It's subtle, but what Coase proposed was to *transform externalities into assets*. This is the same suggestion later made by Frank Popoff, the CEO of Dow Chemical. At the moment, externalities are just *out there,* floating in space, on no one's balance sheet. There are no property rights attached to them, hence no owners, hence no one to pay. But if we turn externalities into assets and attach owners to them, then self-regulating markets can run the show. That this could be done was Coase's great insight.

3. Imagine multiple paths to happiness.

At last we come to the real bottom line—happiness. Economists don't think or write much about happiness. Not that they have anything against it; it's just that the concept is—well, *squishy.* You can't quantify happiness the way you can quantify stuff. And if you can't quantify something, it's not a fit subject for most economists.

What economists do talk about, occasionally, is *utility.* Utility means, more or less, *usefulness.* Ever since Jeremy Bentham, the nineteenth-century apostle of utilitarianism, the mission of economics has been to create the most utility for the most people. Of course, it's also pretty hard to quantify usefulness. But economists get around this problem by means of a tautology: The utility of a product is, by definition, whatever people will pay for it.

The hypothesis underlying the entire utilitarian edifice is then this: Market transactions add to everyone's utility. The seller gains utility or s/he wouldn't sell. The buyer gains utility or s/he wouldn't buy. Consequently, the more market transactions there are, the more utility is created. Commerce is good. More commerce is better.

This sounds so logical it's easy to forget what we've just discussed: that commerce creates illth as well as utility. I'll return to the illth problem shortly. My point here is that commerce, however useful it may be, *isn't the sole source of happiness.* There are multiple paths to happiness. In some countries, many people find happiness in meditation and service. Within the United States, people sometimes find happiness in work and consuming, but often they find it elsewhere. We're happy hanging out with friends and family, hiking, running, playing baseball, listening to music, gardening, and making pots. We're happy when our stress is low and we're engaged in creative or helpful activity. We may be happy doing less remunerative work than we do in our full-time jobs.

The availability of many paths to happiness is a blessing. The trouble is that our economy steadfastly encourages only one path to happiness: acquisition of more stuff, usually by working and spending more. This is what the market tells us to do, day after day, ad after ad. If we want to feel better, we must buy this product. Nobody *needs* Nike sneakers, Coca-Cola in cans, or Calvin Klein underwear, but through constant barraging we're made to *feel* our need satisfaction (if not happiness) depends on buying, consuming, and displaying them.

Let me be clear about happiness. Happiness is a blend of need satisfaction coming from outside and individual attitude coming from within. Ultimately, all of us are responsible for our own happiness. But economies intrude on our individual quests for happiness, both positively and negatively. When helpful, an economy satisfies some needs from outside and allows time for pursuit of other needs. When unhelpful, it foments needs that can't be met and diminishes our ability to meet genuine needs.

Here I must introduce a concept from beyond economics—what psychologist Abraham Maslow called a "hierarchy of needs." Writing in the 1960s, Maslow argued that human needs arise in an ordered way, with certain needs preceding others. The first needs we experience are *survival* needs: for air, water, food, shelter, sleep, and physical safety. When these needs are met, we begin to experience *social* needs: for love, companionship, acceptance, and respect. Finally, there are moments in our lives when we feel *inner* needs: for meaning, answers to deep questions, closeness to nature or God. (I've altered Maslow's terminology somewhat, but you get the idea.)

Intuitively, Maslow's hierarchy of needs makes sense—a hungry man needs food, not a religious experience. It also demolishes a standard economic assumption. Thus, useful physical products, available through commerce, do a decent job of satisfying *survival* needs, but notice what happens as we move up the needs hierarchy. Once our survival needs are met, *the marginal utility of more stuff declines.* (By "marginal" utility I mean the usefulness of each new unit of stuff.) Higher needs aren't satisfied so much by physical products as by social relations and inner work. The best thing an economy can do to satisfy these needs is to give us time and quietude to pursue them. But this is precisely what our current economy *doesn't* do. It keeps giving us low marginal utility stuff, and shouting at us to buy it. Not only does the stuff not satisfy our higher needs; the shouting deprives us of time and serenity, and generates a kind of permanent *dis*satisfaction, a hard-to-shake feeling that whatever we have, it's not enough.

Another way to paint this picture is to consider how economies evolve. An economy starts out poor and grows richer. At the beginning, it's what I'd call a *shortage* economy; at some later date, if it's lucky, it becomes a *surplus* economy. The differences between these two stages are striking.

In a shortage economy, demand is plentiful and supply is scarce. People want to buy more than the economy can produce. Lines are long and shelves are bare. In a surplus economy, things are reversed. There's no limit to what the economy can produce; the problem is finding buyers for all the stuff that can be churned out. A sizeable chunk of GDP is spent to *make us want* this unneeded output. The unspoken deal upon which the surplus economy rests is "I'll buy your junk if you'll buy mine." This means most people have jobs and credit cards, but also that their higher needs are rarely satisfied.

SHORTAGE vs. SURPLUS ECONOMIES

In shortage economies	*In surplus economies*
Demand exceeds supply	Supply exceeds demand
Supply must be stimulated	Demand must be stimulated
Credit is scarce	Credit is plentiful
Time is plentiful	Time is scarce
Products address survival needs	Products address higher needs
Product lives are long	Product lives are short
Marginal value of stuff is high	Marginal value of stuff is low

Figure 14

Time Poverty

It almost goes without saying that many rules that work in shortage economies won't work in surplus economies. For example, consider the relationship between happiness and time.

Time is, of course, naturally scarce—there are only twenty-four hours in a day, and so many days in our lives. Surplus economies compound this natural scarcity by gobbling up much of the time we're given. As German economist Wolfgang Sachs has written, "Beyond a certain threshold, many things become thieves of time. Goods have to be chosen, bought, set up, used, experienced, maintained, tidied away, dusted, repaired, stored, and disposed of. Likewise, appointments have to be sought, coordinated, agreed upon, put into the diary, maintained, assessed and followed up. Even the most beautiful objects and most valuable interactions gnaw away at our time, the most restricted of all resources."

As disparate and personal as the many paths to happiness are, they all have one thing in common: *They all require more time outside the labor market.* Most Americans—and certainly most well-off Americans—would choose more time outside the labor market and less time inside it, *if* they had the choice. But by and large, we don't have that choice. One reason is that the labor market is notoriously rigid. It's set up for full-time, forty-hour-a-week jobs at factories and offices, with the majority of these jobs running the same eight hours a day, five days a week. Vacations are short, and outside academia, paid sabbaticals and unpaid leaves of absence are rare. Americans who don't like this time rigidity can become part-time workers or independent contractors—and millions do. But the price they pay for this flexibility is high: loss of health and retirement benefits, loss of security, and often a loss of income disproportional to the time gained.

Rigidity of the labor market isn't the only reason most Americans are time-poor. Another is that we lack property income. This, more than anything else, is what binds us to the relentless clock of the labor market. If enough of us had enough property income, we'd be less driven to sell our time. We'd sell less of it, and ask more for what we sell—and the labor market would adjust accordingly.

This is where new property rights come in. Property, if you happen to own some, is a wonderful source of income. The trouble is, most income-producing property is owned by a small percentage of the population. But what if we "assetized" externalities and assigned them to everyone through a set of trusts? Pollution, and perhaps other forms of illth, would go down. But just as important, *everyone would have a source of property income.* There'd be no guarantees, of course—the flow of property income would vary from year to year. But as more externalities were turned into assets, everyone's property income would rise. We could use this income to buy more time—and, I'd venture, more happiness as well. The full potential of surplus economies might then be realized.

4. Imagine new economic plumbing.

Thus far we've talked about the scarcity of sinks, the pricing of externalities, and the pursuit of happiness. Now it's time to add a fourth object of consideration: money pipes.

Let's begin our last thought experiment with a tale of two games—a card game called *Capitalism* and a board game called *Monopoly.*

The card game was taught to me several years ago by my brother-in-law. It's best played with seven or more players, so it's perfect for family get-togethers. Two or more decks are shuffled together. To start the game, everyone draws a card. The drawn cards determine the initial pecking order—one through seven, or the total number of players. Pecking order is very important in this game. In fact, it's the whole point.

Everyone now sits around the table in clockwise pecking order. Cards are dealt. The player at the bottom of the pecking order must pass his three highest cards to the player at the top; in exchange, the top player returns her three worst cards. Similarly, the second player from the bottom passes her two highest cards to the second player from the top, in exchange for that player's two worst cards. Likewise for the third players from the bottom and top. Then, play begins. The object of the game is to work yourself up to the top of the pecking order.

I'll skip the details of actual play because you can already see what's so true to life about this game. It's very hard to dislodge the top dogs because, by dint of their inherited positions, they start off with the bottom dogs' best cards.

The second game, *Monopoly,* is familiar to practically all Americans. It's the capitalist game *par excellence,* with players buying and selling property and trying to build little monopolies. But there are two rules of *Monopoly* that make it very different from real-life capitalism. First, all players receive the same amount of start-up capital. And second, all players receive a cash infusion when they complete a trip around the board.

What do these games have to do with money pipes? Two things. These games show, first of all, that there's more than one way to plumb a capitalist economy. You can start everyone off equally, or you can start people with widely varying inheritances. Either way, the capitalist engine runs just fine.

Second, *Monopoly* shows how nonlabor income, received on the same basis by everyone, can enliven a capitalist system. In *Monopoly,* all players regularly get $200 for passing Go, and that helps them buy property and become better capitalists.

Now, on to the last experiment. Money, like water and carbon, flows in circles. It flows *from* people based on what they spend and save, and *to* people based on what they inherit and earn. For purposes of this experiment, let's imagine money flows through pipes.

Let's talk about inheritance pipes first. Experts such as John Havens and Paul Schervish of Boston College say American baby boomers are poised to inherit some $40 trillion in private assets from their parents, the largest intergenerational wealth transfer ever. Most members of the departing generation—let's call them Depression Babies—would like their children to believe their inheritance flows from decades of parental toil. The truth, however, is that the Depression Babies were lucky.

After a shaky start, Depression Babies enjoyed half a century of uninterrupted prosperity and growth. Houses and stock they bought in the 1950s and 1960s rose exponentially in value. Of the trillions they're passing on, most derives not from their own labor, but from the appreciation of assets they bought and held. That they amassed such a sizeable kitty is, thus, more a historical phenomenon than a sum of individual feats.

There's also the matter of precisely who gets the $40 trillion. There are about 78 million baby boomers today. If the Depression Babies' estate were divided equally, each boomer would inherit about $513,000. Personally, I'd be happy if someone walked in the door and handed me a check for $513,000. But of course, that isn't how it works.

The way it works is, my parents hand *me* checks and your parents hand *you* checks. What that means in practice is that a sizeable chunk of Americans get *no* checks, the majority get small checks, and a tiny minority get huge checks. In other words, though the majority of Americans would do better if we divided the intergenerational kitty equally, we choose to divide it quite unequally. That's how our intergenerational money pipes are now plumbed.

At the moment, however, these intergenerational pipes are connected only to *private* assets. And those, as this book strives to make clear, aren't the only kind. The vast majority of us inherit more *common* assets than the private kind. We're born into communities that have clean water, sewers, roads, garbage collection, schools, and much else, all set up and running. We're born into a nation that has stable political institutions, a strong currency, a sophisticated stock market. We're born into a culture that has the biggest knowledge base that ever existed. And we're born into a biosphere that has just the right sky, just the right gravity, and just the right DNA. *So what* if our parents leave us nothing?

Unfortunately, it matters if our parents leave us nothing. It matters because private assets are *liquid,* and common assets—at least for now— aren't. Private assets can be turned into cash that can be spent and invested. Common assets are good for many things, but not for that. If the real game of capitalism, like the card game, heavily favors players with start-up capital, kids who inherit no private assets are at a big disadvantage.

Let's talk next about earnings pipes, the ones that carry *intra*generational money. There are two sets of intragenerational pipes, one that carries *labor* income and another that carries *property* income. Virtually every household is connected to thin labor income pipes; a small minority is connected to thick property income pipes.

Now imagine a third set of intragenerational pipes that distribute income from common assets that haven't heretofore been liquid. Because these assets belong to everyone, the new pipes flow to everyone, and they're are all the same thickness. In this picture the old labor and property income pipes remain as they are, and the new common asset pipes even things out a bit.

My basic thesis is that sinks and externalities should be converted into assets whose income flows equally to everyone. There are tricks to doing this, just as there are tricks involved in every new product. But it *can* be done. It's certainly no harder starting a mutual fund.

Lessons

We've come a long way in this chapter. Are there any lessons we can draw from mixing all four thought experiments together, as if in a single bowl? Let's review our assumptions:

- Sinks are scarce, so we should pay rent for using them.
- Externalities are consequential, so we should pay for them as we go.
- In surplus economies, marginal happiness depends less upon marginal stuff than upon marginal time.
- Current money pipes are skewed toward owners and inheritors of private assets.

Tossing these assumptions together, we then did a novel but very feasible thing. We took some sinks and externalities and turned them into income-producing assets. Since these were new assets, we assigned them to new owners. And since they were *common* assets, we assigned them to everyone equally. Finally, we let the whole pot stew.

What emerges is a version of capitalism that does less damage to our planet and makes more people happier than does the current version. The key difference is a new set of "assetized" common assets, typically placed in trusts. These new assets fix a lot of old problems. They keep us from destroying our nest. They spur technological innovation. They provide start-up capital and property income to everyone. And they increase happiness.

This new, improved version of capitalism might spawn a reissue of the game *Monopoly* that works like this. As in the old, all players start off equally capitalized and collect equal dividends when they pass Go. In the new game, though, all players take breathers from the action—not in jail, but in shorter workweeks and sabbaticals. They pay monopoly rent to the owner of Boardwalk and Park Place—and scarcity rent to the "No More Free Parking" box that's the source of the Go-passing dividends. A few players win big, hardly any live in poverty, and the game goes on for a very long time.

As a business person and a human, at once competitive and compassionate, I'd love to play a real-world version of *Monopoly* like this. I'd love going to work and thinking, "I'm paying the externalities I create—as are my competitors." I'd love knowing that, thanks to my efforts and others', illth is receding and genuine well-being is increasing. And I'd love trusting that the game I'm playing won't destroy the planet.

Where's the Dark Side?

What about unintended consequences, the dark side, the inevitable illth? Where might they lurk in this vision? Of course there will be some. Prices of certain goods will rise; some jobs will be lost. But those are small, unavoidable transition costs—due not to this new version of capitalism per se, but to such realities as the scarcity of sky.

I must confess I have a hard time seeing much downside in the new capitalism. All the good features of capitalism-as-we-know-it are still there: free markets, dynamism, opportunities for self-advancement. There's no increase in government regulation; in fact, there could be a decrease. Taxes and social insurance would stay pretty much as they are now; the job of reducing inequality would be assigned to markets as well as government. The new rent we'd pay for scarce nature would be offset by efficiencies gained elsewhere in the economy—better information management, faster inventory distribution, greater energy efficiency, smarter traffic systems, higher vehicle occupancies, and so on. The one big change would be the creation of new common property. But since no private property would be taken or taxed away, that doesn't hurt anyone.

In a nutshell, here's how the new system would work. Think back to Figure 10 on page 82, in which the human economy is exploding into nature. Assume a sizeable chunk of the area around the human economy now consists of common assets held in trusts. Picture what then happens.

- Usage limits are set on these common assets—only so much carbon can be put in the sky, so much fresh water removed from the water cycle, so many hormone-distrupting chemicals released into the environment. These limits are set politically, aided by the best available science.

- Prices are charged to use these scarce common assets. The prices arise from selling and buying use permits. They're set by markets, through the balance of supply and demand.

- Businesses trade usage rights amongst each other, so the overall economy uses common assets as efficiently as possible.

- The money received from initial sales of usage rights goes into a variety of trusts. These trusts have clearly defined beneficiaries—in some cases it's all citizens equally, in others it's a nondiscriminatory subset of citizens (such as children or the elderly), or a public good such as education, mass transit, or clean elections. A sizeable amount of money circulates according to the formula, *from* all according to their use of a common asset, *to* all according to their equal ownership.

- People receive enough property income from their shares of common assets that they're able to spend less time in the labor market and more time with families, friends, and nature.

This twenty-first-century upgrade of capitalism avoids the old left/right battles that have paralyzed American politics for years. It draws on conservative *and* liberal ideals, and marries them through an expansion of property rights rather than government. It's pro-family, pro-environment, and market-based. It requires no new taxes and has little effect on the federal budget. Most important, it conserves nature, gives workers a cushion and kids a head start. And once the pieces are in place, it does this all almost *automatically*.

The only tricky part—and it *is* tricky—is designing the new property right. But I've got no doubt that somewhere in our great land is a small but dedicated band of property rights architects. Mix them with some clever lawyers and investment bankers, add a few Jay Hammonds, and we could have a pretty good century.

Chapter 7

The New Commons

I own one share of the corporate Earth, and I'm uneasy
about the management.

—E. B. White

2002
Large Antarctic ice shelf breaks off; Dow reaches 13,000
Carbon dioxide concentration in the air: 380 parts per million
Average temperature at surface of the earth: 58.6°F

W ere I a more verbose writer, this chapter might be titled, "A
Modern Way for Commoners to Own the Commons, or at
Least Parts of It." Obviously, I've chosen brevity over clarity. But the
unused title crisply summarizes what the present chapter is about.

These pages propose to define a new class of common property that
lies somewhere between private property and state property. This class
would include things the ancient Romans called *res communes,* plus
many things the Romans never dreamed of. Broadly speaking, it
would encompass a variety of assets we inherit together, as part of a
community, as distinct from assets we inherit individually. The sum of

the assets in this class—let's call them *common assets*—would constitute an intangible commons.

Unlike the old commons, the new commons would be a patchwork of property rights rather than a plot of land. The distinguishing feature of the assets in the new commons is that they'd be held in trust for everyone equally, and for future generations. In many cases, beneficial ownership would be represented by nontransferable shares acquired at birth, like shares of the Alaska Permanent Fund.

My thesis is simple. *This new class of property is the missing piece that will save capitalism from itself.* It's the *proxy* that capitalism needs to start charging for externalities now priced at zero. And it's the *mechanism* that capitalism needs to discharge its responsibilities to future generations and those without private property.

When discussing this vision of a new commons with friends, I often find myself attacked from both sides of the political spectrum. My liberal friends say, "Wait a minute! You're trying to privatize the commons, turn something sacred into something profane. That's not a good idea. What's more, you downplay the importance of government." My conservative friends say, "Common property makes me nervous. The only good property is individual property." Either way, I'm forced to pour more drinks.

In the interest of sobriety, let me explain what common property is and isn't. It isn't, in the first place, communism. Communism, as I understand it, involves a great deal of *state* ownership but very little *common* ownership. The two are quite distinct. Common ownership is a nonstatist form of ownership that differs from individual ownership only as corporations differ from sole proprietorships. Indeed, the role of corporations in private ownership is filled by trusts in common ownership.

Common property isn't, in the second place, privatization of a commons, at least in the way privatization is generally understood. When a state-owned company, say British Telecom, is "privatized," it's actually made available to the public. (My, how words get abused!) When scholars at the Cato Institute call for "privatizing" Social Security, what they mean is *individualizing* the risk of outliving your savings. Neither of these meanings of "privatization" applies to the common property I'm talking about.

My liberal friends are right about one thing, though: I want to do *something* to the commons. Unfortunately, there's no good English word to describe what that is. Awkwardly, I've used the term "assetization" to connote the process of converting a common inheritance into a form of property recognized by markets. That clunky word captures *some* of what's going on, but not all. Literal assetization—the step in which a previously unowned asset is turned into an asset belonging to *someone*—is just the first step in creating common property. There's then a second step—assigning beneficial ownership to all of us equally; a third step—creating a pricing mechanism; and a fourth step—paying dividends to the new owners. Unfortunately, our language lacks a single word to describe this entire process.

In truth, common property is a hybrid. The Sky Trust *does*, in a sense, privatize the atmosphere's carbon-absorbing capacity—it turns the sky into a source of income for individuals. However, these individuals can't sell their rights to that income. And the asset itself is held in trust for future generations and managed as a coherent entity.

Societal Assets

Up till now, the assets I've proposed to "assetize" have all been gifts of nature. Here I suggest (albeit tentatively) that there may be other assets worth adding to the new commons.

In addition to nature's gifts, we share a vast *societal* inheritance that makes private wealth possible, and thus itself has economic value. We inherit these assets not from the common creation, but from our common ancestors.

The list of such societal assets is large. It includes our languages and cultures, our scientific knowledge, our legal, political, and economic institutions, and even newfangled things like the Internet. The exact value of this societal inheritance, like that of nature, is incalculable. Still, it's safe to say it's enormous. If we had to reinvent music every generation, there'd never be a Mozart or a McCartney. If we had to recreate math and science every few decades, there'd never be cars or computers. If we had to reconstruct our financial system every thirty years, commerce would be greatly hindered. In a word, without our societal inheritance, there'd hardly be civilization, much less millionaires and billionaires.

By saying that much of our wealth is inherited from our collective ancestors, I don't mean to disparage individual effort. As an entrepreneur, I firmly believe in the importance of individual effort. Even if it accounts for only a small percentage of our wealth, it's a *catalytic* percentage, without which the machinery of enterprise would grind to a halt. Frankly, though, we entrepreneurs get more credit than we deserve. It's just as important to recognize the role of societal assets—perhaps even more important, because they get so little respect.

Adam Smith, the father of capitalist economics, was well aware of the value of societal assets. The wealth of modern nations, he observed, is based on the division of labor. Instead of one person making and selling each product, a multitude of people do little tasks that, when artfully coordinated, boost everyone's productivity enormously. The trick is achieving that artful coordination—a task best performed, Smith said, by an *invisible hand.*

But what, in reality, is this famous hand? It's a web of societal assets that took centuries to evolve. It includes an exchange medium (money) that lets you trade with far-flung strangers, a stock market that magically "liquefies" the value of a going business, plus a bevy of inducements and penalties, rules and boundaries, property rights and labor laws, that make markets honest and efficient. When Russians decided to try free enterprise in the 1990s, they discovered that many of these societal assets were missing. Capitalism, they belatedly realized, is a lot more than rugged individualists duking it out on a barren playing field. It requires societal assets as well.

In short, a host of societal assets make up the firmament from which private wealth emerges. This is true both as a general statement applying to nations, and as a particular statement applying to individual fortunes. Consider, for example, the source of the earliest fortunes made in America: land speculation. Land itself is a gift of nature. Its exchange value, however, is a social creation. Land speculators acquire large chunks of undeveloped land at low prices, then wait for the land's exchange value to rise. And what makes that happen? The multiplicity of systems by which society spreads to, inhabits, and develops new territory. A railroad or highway is built. Settlers are lured. Farming, trade, and industry get going. A sheriff is chosen. Schools, churches, water lines, and sewers are built. Banks take deposits and make loans (some with government guarantees). Soon, land values soar, and this socially created value is reaped by the speculator.

Or consider the source of the most recent fortunes made in America: dot-com IPOs (initial public offerings). As I've noted, the Internet is a societal asset. Not only was it invented by government contractors; its infrastructure is a network of wires, switches, and codes whose value lies in the fact that they all talk to each other—a social value *par excellence*. What's more, as we'll see, the dot.commers' fortunes would not be possible without another societal asset, the stock market.

If we agree that societal assets are a fount of private wealth, the next logical question is, Should those who use these assets be required to pay for them, or can they use them for free? This is the same question we asked earlier about the sky. My answer then was that users should pay for sky because it's scarce and we're overusing it. My answer with regard to societal assets is more nuanced.

The argument *against* charging for most societal assets is that there's no need to—they aren't scarce in the same way sky is. The Internet, in theory, can expand indefinitely. So can our knowledge base, our stock markets and our money supply (though we wouldn't want to expand the latter too quickly). On the other hand, when societal assets *are* scarce—as with highways—it may make sense to charge for use and collect the scarcity rent. For example, as highway congestion mounts, a system of congestion pricing seems sensible. Users would pay for the miles they drive, and revenue could be spent on car pool lanes and mass transit.

There are, however, other reasons besides scarcity to charge for societal assets. One is that societal assets need care and tending. Our knowledge base won't grow if we don't educate our children and fund research. Our democracy can't flourish unless we liberate it from special interests. The arts always need extra support. We may want to restore sites of historic importance, or make our public transportation more sky-efficient. In short, we can *invest* more in societal assets if we charge something for using them.

A second reason to charge for societal assets is to offset the maldistribution of private assets. As I noted earlier, roughly 5 percent of Americans now own more income-producing private assets than the other 95 percent combined. In the case of the sky, I argued that charging for use could serve two functions simultaneously. First, it could protect the asset from overuse, and second, it could provide property income to all Americans. In the case of societal assets that aren't scarce, the first function disappears, but pricing can still serve two important goals: investment and equity.

I should note that society *does* capture some socially created wealth through the tax on capital gains. This is a tax, payable when a property is sold, on the rise in value of that property. Typically, this rise in value is due in large part to other people's efforts; the owner has simply bought, passively waited, and sold. (I here exclude owners who are actively involved in their businesses; that, however, is a small minority of American property owners.) Quite appropriately, the federal government and many state governments use the capital gains tax to recapture some of this societally created wealth (which the tax code, appropriately, refers to as "unearned income"). However, the tax paid on capital gains is quite low; it's roughly half the rate paid on wages, rents, and dividends. Why do we tax our active labors more steeply than the passive gains that accrue from other people's labors? Ask your Congress member; there's surely room here for improvement.

Biodiversity

It's time now to put meat on the table. It's time, in this case, to name other assets (besides the sky) that can be part of the new commons. I should warn that some of these assets may surprise you; they're not what you usually think of as assets. (But then, do you usually think of pork belly futures as assets?) Also, some are a bit "derived" (but no more so than the wacky derivatives that trade today). And some will stretch your imagination beyond its present limit (but remember, my goal *is* to stretch your imagination). Forthwith, then, a few suggestions.

Let's begin with the earth's biodiversity—or at least America's piece of it. This requires a bit of history. Humans are one of perhaps ten million species currently occupying the Earth. We all share a common ancestry, genetic language, and biosphere. Until about ten thousand years ago, we also shared constraints on population growth and habitat occupation. Like other species, humans could only occupy habitats with sufficient water, sunlight, and food to keep us alive, and could only reproduce to the extent these habitats permitted.

Then came agriculture. Farming and animal husbandry enabled *homo sapiens* to occupy almost any habitat in the world and to multiply seemingly without limit. Since their invention, the number of humans has soared from five million to over six billion, a thousandfold increase in just a blink of geologic time. And, as we expanded our numbers, farms, factories, and cities, we disturbed over 90 percent of the earth's land area, a good chunk of its rivers and oceans, and even its atmosphere.

As humans spread, other species declined. In the past hundred years, their rate of decline has reached alarming proportions. Scientists estimate that roughly thirty thousand species now vanish every year, while thousands more fall closer to the edge. These species, it should be noted, are among the hardiest ever known—they're survivors of three billion years of brutal competition. Yet they're dying at the fastest rate since the mass extinction that wiped out the dinosaurs.

In the past, mass extinctions (there've been five) are thought to have been caused by cataclysmic events—meteor collisions or huge volcanic eruptions that triggered sudden climatic changes. The present wave of extinctions, by contrast, lacks a cataclysm. Its cause is the human juggernaut—the relentless spread of our bodies and wastes to almost every nook and cranny of the biosphere. This juggernaut has caused an enormous fragmentation and loss of other species' habitats.

If the current rate of extinctions continues, biologists such as Edward O. Wilson predict we'll lose a quarter of the earth's remaining species within the twenty-first century. By contrast, if we slow the extinction rate down, we may be able to hold the loss to 10 percent. The difference is important. The creatures that sustain earthly life are mostly plants and microorganisms that convert solar energy to sugar, enrich the soil, create the oxygen we breathe, and cleanse our wastes. Most of these creatures,

even today, are unknown to us. But it's reasonable to think of them, collectively, as an asset we should preserve.

How this might be done is of course the operative question. The current mode of species preservation is a piecemeal approach: protect a forest here, a wetlands there, and when an especially cute-looking species is
endangered, take heroic measures to save it. I suspect this will soon be
seen as insufficient. I suspect we'll see the need to protect undisturbed
habitat on a much larger scale. At that point, we might wish to assetize
undisturbed habitat, limit total incursions, and allow a market to arise for
the incursions permitted. We might wish, in other words, to create a U.S.
Habitat Trust. How might such a system work?

The first step is to decide exactly what the underlying asset is, and
how to quantify it. In the case of the Sky Trust, we defined the underlying asset as the sky's remaining carbon absorption capacity, and we quan-
tified its use in terms of tons per year. In the case of a Habitat Trust, we
may want to use a derivative—something that doesn't quantify habitat
per se, but is closely linked. For example, because new roads are what ini-
tiate habitat loss, we might define the underlying asset as nature's capacity to absorb new roads—that is, roads that encroach upon minimally
disturbed land.

The connection between roads and habitat loss is well established.
Roads break up habitats into isolated patches. They restrict the movement,
and hence the supply, of food. They affect soil and water content, temperature, and sedimentation. And of course, they attract human settlement,
which brings land use changes, pollution, and noise. As biologists Stephen
Trombulak and Chistopher Frissell note, "Even where only a small percentage of the land's surface is directly occupied by roads, few corners of
the landscape remain untouched by their off-site ecological effects."

Here are some facts about roads in America. Pavement now covers
over 60,000 square miles, which is 10 percent of our arable land. About
1.5 million acres of farmland, plus 50,000 acres of wetlands, are lost to
suburban sprawl each year, encouraged by road-building. To maintain
existing roads in their current poor state would cost $25 billion a year, yet
at present we spend only $13 billion a year on maintenance, and $16 billion a year to build new roads.

With a U.S. Habitat Trust, only a limited number of new road miles could be built in a given year. States, counties, and other road-building entities would bid for the rights to add those miles. This would raise the cost of new roads relative to other transportation investments. The revenue from permit sales, plus the money *not* spent on new roads, could be used to maintain existing roads, improve bike paths, and expand mass transit. New housing and commercial facilities would continue to be built, but within the confines of existing roads. This would be good for inner cities and older suburbs, as well as for biodiversity.

I harbor no illusions that humans are eager to stop paving the earth; the prospects for a Habitat Trust are, at this moment, nonexistent. Yet inevitably, the mass extinction we're now causing will become evident even to untrained eyes. At some point in this century, we'll confront the mortal threat we represent to other species and seek substitutes for the constraints nature once imposed on us. That's when we may declare biodiversity an asset worthy of recognition by markets, and take steps to assetize it.

Quietude

Here's an assignment for you. Step outside, close your eyes, and listen very closely to two things: birds and the background hum. Do this for a minute or two. If you're in a medium-size city, the background hum you never noticed before will soon thunder in your ears. That's the sound level your brain is trained to ignore.

I've done this several times and had the same sensation a different way. I once went walking with a high-tech headset that detects and cancels incoming noise waves. (They actually sell these gizmos at fancy hardware stores for about $100.) The area I walked in was a residential neighborhood about twenty miles from the nearest four-lane highway. I listened without the headphones for the background hum—it was there, but not very loud. Then I put on the magic headset. Suddenly, silence. Peaceful, blissful silence. I took off the headphones and the background hum roared much louder than before. It struck me that I might never experience pure silence in my lifetime.

Quietude is a gift of nature. Until a few generations ago, the only noises filling the air were made by animals, wind, and water. Then along came our cars, car alarms, boom boxes, TVs, sirens, airplanes, jack-hammers, cell phones, and leaf-blowers. Now silence, like sky, is scarce.

The scarcity of quietude isn't just an aesthetic concern. It's a genuine health problem—exposure to high noise levels has been linked to hearing loss, sleep disorders, hypertension, learning disabilities, heart disease, mood disturbance, and other afflictions. Certainly, it diminishes peace of mind and worker productivity. And it places significant costs on individuals and society as a whole. The Noise Pollution Clearinghouse states: "Polluting the commons is not a right. Our effort to reduce noise pollution is similar to other efforts to reduce pollution and reassert our collective stewardship over the commons."

What can be done? We could set up a system similar to the Sky Trust. We could establish a Plimsoll line (an ambient decibel level) beyond which quietude couldn't be diminished, and then sell noise emission permits up to the threshold. Each manufacturer of noise-making machines would have to purchase permits equal to the number of machines it sold times the noise-making capacity of each. Within a decade or so, I'd bet, our neighborhoods would be noticeably quieter, and revenue could go into a pot for dividends, or for the arts.

There's another threat to quietude that's of growing concern: the incessant clamor of advertising. Every day we're bombarded by thousands of mercantile demands for our attention. Billboards battle for our gaze outdoors, TVs and computers for our indoor stares. Telemarketers jostle our telephones, catalogs flood our mailboxes, and logos accost us everywhere. Kalle Lasn, editor of *AdBusters* and a former ad man, says, "Our mental environment is a common property resource like the air or the water. We need to protect ourselves from unwanted incursions into it."

The problem, once again, is a scarcity unrecognized by markets. Though demand for our attention inexorably rises, our supply of attention is inherently limited. It's constrained by two factors that are quintessentially scarce: time and brain capacity. There are only twenty-four hours in a day, and we sleep for a third of them. Even when we're awake, there's only so much sensory input our brains can handle. The more our brains are filled with commercial stimuli, the less room we have for love, gratitude, and contentment.

In fact, there's a tragedy of the commons here. Every advertisement, to be seen or heard above the din, must be louder or more eye-grabbing than its competitors. Thus, every new ad slightly raises the background noise level. Eventually the din becomes unbearable.

Here I'll make an assertion I think most people know to be true: The steady rise in noise—both audible and commercial—is making us less content. It's a source of bodily, mental, and spiritual illth. It adds stress and anxiety to our lives. It devalues, if it doesn't completely eliminate, the considerable contentment that can arise from quietude. If the mission of our economy is to maximize contentment rather than sales, there's clearly a flaw here that needs to be fixed.

That fix could begin by thinking of quietude as a common asset we need to preserve. Then, just as we limit the input of carbon into our economy, so could we limit the input of commercial solicitation. In practice, we could do this in a couple of ways.

The simplest and most ancient way is to honor the Sabbath as the God of Moses commanded. The point of the Sabbath, let's recall, isn't just to refrain from working; it's also to renew our spirits and family bonds. This can't easily be accomplished amidst a cacophony of demands for attention and money. Why not draw a line around one twenty-four-hour period each week and say, "During this time, to protect quietude, no advertising will be permitted. Stores, cafes, and restaurants can stay open, but they can't advertise. Billboards, if lit, will be turned off. You can still watch football on TV, but the breaks will be filled with public service announcements." I don't think businesses would suffer. They'd just step up their advertising on other days of the week.

The second approach is more flexible, and therefore more complicated. It involves setting limits on commercial use of shared sight and sound space, and then renting that shared space to advertisers. For example, billboards could be limited to a given number per mile of highway or street; TV and radio ads could be limited to so many minutes per hour or day; telemarketing calls, direct mail, and Internet banners could also be capped. The common asset we'd be protecting isn't a particular communications medium, but the finite capacity of our brains to absorb marketing noise. Thus, in addition to paying the owners of various media to run their ads, advertisers would also have to purchase "quietude infringement permits" from a trust. The scarcity rent thus collected could be added to the citizen dividend pot. The less commercial we kept our common spaces, the bigger our dividends would be. Another tragedy of the commons would be averted, and we'd be calmer, healthier, and more content.

Democracy

Doris Haddock, a ninety-year-old grandmother who walked across America to promote campaign finance reform, recently summed up the state of America's democracy: "The running of a democracy requires that we all find out everything we can about each candidate. When I was a young girl, the townspeople would gather around to hear speeches in the park. No one minded if the town paid for the stage or the refreshments. If today's public speaking platforms are the television and the radio, then let's use them as public platforms indeed. The sooner we enable candidates to approach the public directly, without the necessity of ingratiating themselves to the monied interests, the sooner we'll return politics to the human scale where it belongs."

Granny D, as she became known, is on to something. Our democratic political system is among our most valuable common assets. It's valuable to *everyone* because it preserves freedom, domestic tranquility, and government accountability. The trouble is, it's also valuable to business interests because it dispenses a lot of industry-specific benefits. This in itself would not be a problem were it not for the fact that politicians nowadays are desperate for large sums of money. They need the money mostly for TV ads, and they must go to business interests to get it. Consequently, it's businesses' desires for favored treatment, not citizens' common needs, that our democracy increasingly attends to.

The irony is that the root of the problem lies in the giveaway of another common asset, the airwaves. "The airwaves are the inalienable possession of the people," declared the legislative history of the Radio Act of 1927. Yet today, less than a dozen media corporations effectively own most of the broadcast frequencies. In practice, their licenses are renewed indefinitely and periodically sold for billions of dollars. The public benefit, if any, is slight.

What happened? We, the owners of the airwaves, gave them to private broadcasters at no charge. Now our elected representatives must pay these recipients of public largesse for the privilege of communicating (via advertisements) with ourselves. Our elected representatives then bend to special interests to get the money to do this.

If we reclaimed our common assets, this is what we'd do. We'd require broadcasters, as a condition of holding a free license, to let us use a small percentage of our own airwaves to conduct elections—the gift we've already given them more than compensates. Alternatively, we'd charge broadcasters for using our airwaves, and devote the revenue to financing political campaigns. Taxes then wouldn't finance elections, but spectrum rental would. Either way, we'd get our democracy back, and that would be a priceless gain.

Liquidity

A few pages back, I talked about the billions of dollars that have lately befallen dot-com entrepreneurs. I noted that their rapid rise to riches could not have occurred without a valuable societal asset, the Internet. And indeed this is so. But the Internet isn't the only societal asset that rains bounty on billionaires. A much older societal asset has been doing this for decades. It's called the stock market.

The stock market, as I mean it here, is a generic term for any arena where stock in public companies is traded, subject to public rules. Public companies are "public" in two ways. First, any member of the public can buy their stock, no questions asked. And second, important information about them must be reported to the Securities and Exchange Commission, which makes that information available to the public.

Every weekday, the stock of public companies moves in and out of the portfolios of millions of investors. As the stock moves, some people make money and others lose. Though the media's attention focuses on this daily casino, the casino is, by itself, of little consequence. Of far greater import is the simple fact that public stock is *liquid.*

Liquidity is a very nice thing. This was brought home to me several years ago when Working Assets considered going public. We retained an investment banker to appraise what the company was worth. What we, the private shareholders, learned, was that our business was worth a whole lot more as a public company than as a private company. What added this extra value? It wasn't that we'd make more sales or profit as a public company—these numbers would be the same either way. The extra value came purely from the fact that our stock would be *liquid*—we could sell it to any Tom, Dick, or Harriet, any day of the week. According to our investment banker, liquidity alone would add 30 percent to the value of our stock. And that was *before* the crazy stock market of the late nineties, when companies that went public could multiply their value overnight.

In the end, we decided not to take Working Assets public. We knowingly "left money on the table" because we didn't want to lose our independence or integrity. But the lesson I learned has stuck in my brain ever since: *Liquidity alone accounts for 30 percent of a public company's value,* perhaps even more. That added value comes not from the company itself, but from society—from the stock market and the infrastructure of government, financial institutions, and media that supports it. Yet this socially created wealth is reaped by only two kinds of people: underwriters (who get fees) and private shareholders (who get capital gains). Indeed, it's fair to say that most fortunes in America are amassed by shareholders who make the magic leap from illiquid private stock to liquid public stock. Though the socially created value of liquidity is in theory available to all, it truly enriches only a few.

Think now about the market value of publicly traded American companies. If 30 percent of that is attributable to the value added by liquidity, we're staring at a societal asset worth trillions.

How might the value of this asset be more broadly shared? Imagine that every time a private company goes public, it pays not only a fee to its underwriters, but also a royalty to the public for using our commonly inherited liquidity system. This royalty could be paid in cash, or quite possibly in stock. Personally, I like the idea of a giant mutual fund—call it USA Inc.—which holds, say, 5 percent of the stock of all publicly traded companies. The shareholders of this mutual fund would be every American—one citizen, one share. Shares would be nontransferable until each citizen reached age sixty-five. Then USA Inc. would redeem them at market value, giving everyone an extra nest egg for retirement. With such a universal mutual fund, a rising tide would automatically lift all boats. What's good for the Dow would, quite literally, be good for all Americans.

A Single Annual Statement

Here, as a business person, I must interject something. I *hate* transaction costs. I hate paying lawyers, bankers, and middle-people of all sorts who rearrange, but don't really add to, wealth. If there's any way to lower transaction costs, I'm for it. I therefore like the idea of having many common asset trusts, but just one common assets statement.

This may sound like a detail, but I want to be quite concrete about what the new commons could look like. The patchwork of common asset trusts would have a central clearinghouse. All dividends would be reported to the clearinghouse and paid through it (much the way VISA and MasterCard work, but a whole lot simpler). Once a year, the clearinghouse would electronically transfer funds to each citizen's bank or brokerage account, where the combined "citizen's dividend" would show up as a lump sum. The clearinghouse would also mail to each citizen (via both "snail mail" and the Internet) a consolidated annual report, with financial statements of all common asset trusts. These reports would explain how the common assets are being managed and how the interests of future generations are being protected. Quite possibly, they'd contain a consolidated statement like that seen in Figure 16.

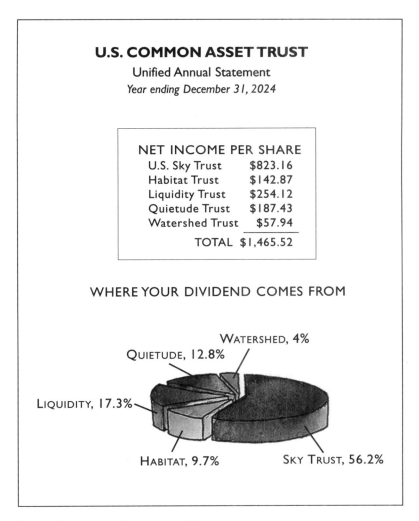

Figure 15. Consolidated Annual Statement

Creating the New Commons

The new commons won't be built overnight. It could take the better part of a century to construct it, asset by asset, starting with a Sky Trust and ending who knows where.

Beginning the century with a Sky Trust would not only help stabilize

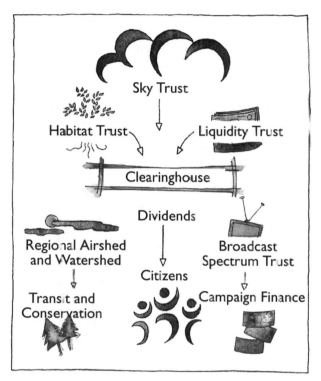

Figure 16. The Common Sector
The common sector would consist of a variety of trusts, each charging for private use of a common asset. Money earned by the trusts would flow to citizens through a clearinghouse, or to specific public goods.

the climate; it would legitimate a number of important new political principles, including the following:

- Beneficial ownership of a common asset can be functionally separated from usage rights.
- The people, collectively, can beneficially own a common asset.
- The interests of future generations can be legally protected.
- Income from common assets is a birthright of all citizens.
- Such income should be allocated on a one citizen, one share basis.

What happens after a Sky Trust is established is of course impossible to foresee. If these new principles catch on, I can imagine a mid-twenty-first-century New Deal—a burst of creativeness from which emerges an alphabet soup not of new federal agencies, but of common asset trusts. As more gifts of nature become scarce, more scarcity rent would flow through these trusts' pipes. There could be a proliferation of regional trusts for airsheds and watersheds, focusing on pollutants that remain local. There could be an Intergenerational Transfer Trust replacing the estate and gift tax, with income flowing equally to all babies. The "common sector" of the U.S. economy could grow to 10 percent of GDP, and common asset property income to perhaps 10 percent of labor income.

Just as social insurance was one of the great achievements of the twentieth century, the new commons, in its various manifestations, could be a legacy of the twenty-first. Whereas social insurance mainly helps people late in life, the fruits of common assets would help people early in life and throughout life. Such assets wouldn't just be safety nets, they'd also be ladders. They'd temper the maldistribution of private wealth without disturbing it, increase individual and family security, and provide hope and opportunity where those have been lacking. And unlike public assistance, they'd come as a part of American citizenship, with no means testing and no bureaucrats asking questions.

The new commons would also let us—indeed, *compel* us—to hold common assets in trust for future generations. When properly priced, the assets would generate income for the living, but the trusts would also be bound to preserve, if not enhance, the assets for generations to come. If there was ever a conflict between current income and asset preservation, the trusts would have to side with asset preservation. There's no rocket science required here; this is exactly what private trusts do all the time. Over time, both the value of our common assets and the income derived from them could rise.

In short, the new commons would be a set of wealth managing trusts, governed by trustees and accountable to citizens. These asset-holding trusts would represent unrepresented generations and ecosystems in real-time market transactions (albeit imperfectly), and perhaps make our political system more democratic as well.

Not least of all, they'd connect our present, past, and future in a meaningful way. We, the living, often pay lip service to our ancestors and grandchildren, but we lack institutions to turn our rhetoric into meaningful behavior. Corporations are driven by quarterly profit statements, governments by the next election. How nice it would be if *one* sector of our economy had a multigenerational time horizon! The new commons would do this.

Chapter 8

Capitalism 2.0

Studies of the Kalahari bushmen of Africa indicate that hunter gatherers—the men doing the hunting and the women doing the gathering—work about two or three days a week, spending the rest of their time socializing, sleeping, dancing, visiting, being hosts, telling stories, playing with children, and making music.
—Paul Shepard

The least a government could do, it seems to me, is to divide things up fairly among the babies.
—Kurt Vonnegut

2020
Hurricane Britney devastates Miami; Sky Trust dividend is $1,017.
Carbon dioxide concentration in the air: 422 parts per million
Average temperature at surface of the earth: 59.3°F

Adam Smith wasn't often wrong, but he erred in thinking the invisible hand would work forever without updated instructions. The world has changed, and it's time for a software upgrade. If Bill Gates can do it every three years for Windows, we can surely do it every generation or so for capitalism.

Let me nurse my metaphor a bit. Capitalism, like a computer, requires an operating system. In my Macintosh, the operating system coordinates the keyboard and mouse, the short-term memory, long-term memory, monitor, modem, and printer. In capitalism, the operating system coordinates workers, investors, managers, and consumers all over the globe. Its code is written in many legislatures and courtrooms, a little at a time—in this regard, it's more like Linux than Windows.

The operating system of capitalism isn't a bad one, except for a few stubborn flaws. Bugs, you might call them. Because of these flaws, common assets such as the sky are degraded. Because of these flaws, one of five American children is born into poverty, with slim odds of escaping. Because of these flaws, species go extinct. Thus the need for an upgrade.

This book shows how we can upgrade capitalism gracefully, by which I mean gradually, fairly, and transparently. The virtues of gracefulness, I'd add, are many. Fewer people get hurt. Solidarity is strengthened. From an economic perspective, less money is lost and more money can be made. Graceful upgrading is good for GDP *and* genuine well-being.

The big problem with graceful upgrading is getting it started. It's much easier to react to unexpected crises than to avert foreseeable ones. Almost by definition, gracefulness is anticipatory. It requires action while there's still time to be gradual, changing before we're *forced* to change. And this necessitates a leap of faith.

I sense that, on the matter of stabilizing the climate, most Americans are ready to make a leap of faith, *if* the pain to them is minimized. Most Americans know, at some level, that we're playing with fire when we double the greenhouse gases in the atmosphere. The reason we dillydally is that we don't see how we can break our carbon-burning habit without pain.

A Sky Trust gives us reason to stop procrastinating; it offers plenty of pain protection and dividends for everyone. But a Sky Trust does more. It opens the door to other upgrades in capitalism that gracefully fix its software flaws. Here's how.

Citizen-Shareholders

I was once at a conference where an executive of DuPont was asked why his company didn't do more to protect the environment. His response was, "Any company that doesn't respect shareholder value doesn't do anyone any good."

Yes, I thought, that's true. But aren't we all shareholders in something larger than a single corporation—and don't we have to protect *that* shareholder value, too? I began to imagine a giant holding company, Earth Holdings Inc., that owned the sky, the oceans, the fresh-water replenishment system, DNA, and other common assets. The shareholders of Earth Holdings Inc. were every human equally. Their—or rather *our*—concern for shareholder value pushed management to charge market prices for use of Earth's assets. The result was that our assets were well cared for. A side effect was that money flowed from overusers of Earth's assets to underusers.

The trouble with capitalism, I realized, is that it lacks an Earth Holdings Inc. It has millions of private corporations pursuing *their* shareholders' interests, but none protecting the more numerous shareholders of Earth. Hence, private assets are always maximized at the expense of common assets. Hence, short-term profits trump the interests of future generations. A countervailing set of shareholders, to borrow John Kenneth Galbraith's term, is wanting.

Who could those shareholders be? Well, why not you, me, and our heirs? Or, to put it more generically, why not all current and future citizens? It's only a matter of defining clear property rights.

When we upgrade capitalism, the new, improved operating system—let's call it Capitalism 2.0—will have lots of whiz-bang features. But its main selling points will a new set of shareholders (all of us equally) and a new sector of the economy I've called the *common sector*. This is a sector that didn't exist in earlier versions. (Actually, it existed *before* capitalism, but one of capitalism's early code changes was to eliminate it.) The role of the common sector in Capitalism 2.0 isn't to run the show—that job is still performed by the private sector. The role of the common sector, with its new citizen-shareholders, is to lengthen the private sector's time horizons and offset its inequities.

Like the private sector, the common sector in Capitalism 2.0 is decentralized—*distributed,* as code writers say. The role of corporations in the private sector is played by trusts in the common sector. Each trust manages its own common asset and has its own trustees; each deals with a distinct market, region, or industry. There are trusts for America's shares of global carbon-absorption capacity, habitat diversity, and geostationary satellite slots; there are trusts for quietude, liquidity, and the broadcast spectrum; and there are trusts for regional ecosystems such as watersheds and airsheds. Most of the mechanical work done for these trusts—auctioning, trading, record keeping, and dividend paying—is done by firms in the private sector.

The primary source of money in the common sector is scarcity rent. This is the rent charged for using scarce but previously unpriced common assets. It's money that didn't exist before. It isn't *tax* money—that is, money taken out of the private sector and put into the state sector. It's money paid in markets to the inheritors of common assets, who happen to be all of us. It's money that quickly returns to the private sector, where it's invested or spent.

If we were to make a chart of the sectors in Capitalism 2.0, in which each sector was defined by its from/to formula, this is what we'd see in Figure 17.

Sector	Key Institution	From Each According to	To Each According to
Labor	Individual worker	Use	Hours worked, skill, bargaining power
Capital	Corporation	Use	Ownership
Public services	Government	Tax liability	Use
Transfer payments	Government	Tax liability	Need
Social insurance	Trust fund	Wages	Disability, unemployment, longevity
Common assets	Trust	Use	Ownership

Figure 17. Capitalism 2.0: Sectors and Their Money Recycling Formulas

In operation, money would cycle in and out of each sector in accordance with its from/to formula. Thus, an imaginary dollar might flow via a paycheck from an employer (who uses labor) to a worker (based on his or her time worked, skill, and bargaining power). If the worker then spends this dollar on a jar of mayonnaise, this sends the dollar back to a corporation which uses it to pay a wage-based Social Security contribution. The dollar then moves through the Social Security trust fund to a retired widow, who uses it to pay her rent. And so on.

Of course, any given dollar might move anywhere, or be divided amongst several sectors, companies, and/or individuals. My point is that the distribution of dollars within the economy depends on the from/to formulas within each sector and how many dollars flow through that sector. As more dollars move through the common sector—with its one-person, one-share ownership structure—the income gap between rich and poor would narrow.

It's worth noting that the incentives driving Capitalism 2.0 are no different from those driving the present operating system. Humans are still spurred by self-interest rather than altruism. Corporations still seek to maximize their return on investment. What's different is the way Capitalism 2.0 channels the self-interest of individuals and firms. By charging for using the commons, it penalizes polluters and rewards those who pollute less. Thus, players don't even have to know the software's been changed. All they need to do is keep playing by the rules they're accustomed to.

Keynes's Dream—And Mine

John Maynard Keynes, the great twentieth-century economist, is best remembered for two things: his quip that "in the long run, we're all dead," and his efforts to save capitalism from the scourge of unemployment. His monumental work, *The General Theory of Employment, Interest and Money*, argues that markets, when left to themselves, don't automatically generate work for everyone—governments have to "prime the pump" if enough jobs are to be created. This insight, though radical at first, soon became conventional wisdom. Even Richard Nixon proclaimed, "We're all Keynesians now."

Less well known is the fact that Keynes did have a longer view. In a remarkable essay entitled "Economic Possibilities for our Grandchildren," Keynes wrote in 1930: "Assuming no important wars and no important increase in population, the *economic problem* may be solved, or be at least within sight of solution, within a hundred years. . . . Then, for the first time since his creation, man will be faced with his real, his permanent problem—how to use his freedom from pressing economic cares, how to occupy the leisure which science and compound interest will have won for him, to live wisely and agreeably and well." At that point, Keynes believed, the mindless pursuit of wealth would be shunned, and people would devote themselves to the art of living.

"But beware!" Keynes warned at the essay's end. "The time for all this is not yet. For at least another hundred years we must pretend to ourselves and to everyone that fair is foul and foul is fair, for foul is useful and fair is not. Avarice and usury and precaution must be our gods for a little longer. For only they can lead us out of the tunnel of economic necessity into daylight."

There, in a nutshell, is the Faustian deal millennial capitalism offers us. On the one hand, it promises to liberate us from pressing economic cares. Yet, it also tells us that if we want to reach this nirvana, we must be mean and greedy for a while longer.

If I may dare to say so, the missing piece in Keynes's long view is how we get from greed to gentility. Surely it's one of the tasks of surplus economies to accomplish this, but neither Keynes nor anyone else has figured out how. The idea that a revolution can impose gentility has, I think, been universally abandoned. Other potential change agents include cool technology, spiritual awakening, and more responsible business leadership. Would that they sufficed.

As I said at the start of this book, after leaving Working Assets I contemplated how capitalism might be gracefully fixed. It can't, I came to see, be fixed one company at a time—the incentives aren't right, and there just isn't time for that. It must be fixed *all* companies and consumers together. But how can we engineer such systemic change? What's our tool? What's our technique?

Changing capitalism isn't about changing human nature; it's about inserting code into the current operating system that defines new property rights and boundaries. Boundaries, let's be clear, are nothing new or noxious. There are speed limits on highways, occupancy limits in elevators, height limits on buildings, and parking limits on streets, not to mention minimum wages for workers and Plimsoll lines on ships. None of these inhibits capitalism in any way. Nor would the creation of property rights in common assets.

As I've argued, we can install new economic code gracefully, in a manner that ruffles almost no one. And we can do it without ridding ourselves of avarice. The key is to build a common sector, piece by piece, trust by trust. Each new piece adds previously ignored externalities to the cost of goods sold, and makes property income flow to all citizens, or to public goods like education, transit, and democracy. In this step-by-step way, we can attain, if not the imagined bliss of the Kalahari, at least an enlightened form of capitalism that respects nature and a fuller range of human aspirations.

Let me sum up. Our task as stewards of creation (if not us, who?) is to preserve an irreplaceable yet ill-defined commons. This commons is more than a bunch of obvious things like pasture for sheep or fish in the ocean—it's a set of natural and societal systems that are critical to our well-being. Given the prevalence and efficiency of markets, it seems best to protect this commons *through* markets. Capitalism 2.0, as I envision it, would do this. It would define the commons clearly, with property rights and boundaries markets respect. It would assign these property rights to trusts representing all present and future citizens. These trusts would counterbalance the short-term profit-maximizing of corporations. They'd add to our current economic formulas a new set of calculations. If you use the commons, you pay. As a co-owner of the commons, you get dividends. If you're modest in your use of the commons, you come out ahead. If you're profligate, you come out behind.

In Capitalism 2.0, every baby would be a trust fund baby. When they enter adulthood, their parents could have small nest eggs to give them. No longer will poverty be passed from one generation to the next. Every player of the game of capitalism would start out, if not equally endowed, at least with a modest sum of assets behind them.

It's true that the road ahead seems daunting. But consider the alternatives. One is to continue down the road we're now on, daring nature—and billions of left-behind humans—to seek revenge. That path, I firmly believe, is too risky. A second possibility is to recognize that nature is scarce and getting scarcer. That would unleash a rising flow of scarcity rent, ready to be inherited. Who might the inheritors be? My hope is that they'd be all of us.

In any event, the battle will soon be joined. In the not-very-distant future, many of our common assets will be claimed by *someone*. Either citizens together will claim them, or a small group of corporations will. Trillions of dollars are at stake, and they won't be ignored.

Keynes's vision for his grandchildren may well be attainable by ours. Though such a future is hardly guaranteed, it *is* possible to imagine, as a legacy of my generation, a new operating system for capitalism that protects the commons and broadens property ownership. It's possible to envision a future that works—and a graceful, largely painless way to get there. That, at any rate, is my compassionate businessman's dream, a dream that would be good for the stock market *and* for every living creature.

Appendix 1

Key Features of a U.S. Sky Trust

- Carbon emissions cap is set intially at 1.3 billion tons, the 1990 level.
- Tradeable carbon emission permits are sold annually to energy companies at the top of the carbon chain.
- All revenue from permit sales goes into a nationwide trust.
- The trust pays equal annual dividends to all U.S. citizens (like the Alaska Permanent Fund).
- Dividends can be placed tax-free in Individual Retirement Accounts or Individual Development Accounts for children.
- The initial price ceiling on carbon emission permits is set at $25 a ton; the ceiling rises 7 percent a year for four years.
- A ten-year transition Fund helps those most adversely affected by higher carbon prices. The fund starts at 25 percent of permit revenue, then declines 2.5 percent per year.

Appendix 2

Free Ownership Certificate

You can learn more about the campaign to create a U.S. Sky Trust—and get a free Certificate of Ownership—by logging on to *www. skyowners.org*. The certificate represents your non-transferable share of America's share of the earth's atmosphere. It entitles you to one vote in the election of trustees, an annual report on the State of the Sky, and annual dividends once they begin.

Notes

For specific books, articles, and studies referred to in the text, please see the Bibliography. These Notes contain additional thoughts about the text, and suggestions for further reading.

Introduction: The Wealth Around Us

Page 1   The average surface temperature data, here and at the beginning of all chapters, is from the NASA Goddard Institute for Space Studies Web site <http://www.giss.nasa.gov/data/update/gistemp/GLB.Ts.txt>. The carbon dioxide concentrations for years before 1958 are taken from Etheridge et al.'s study of Antarctic ice cores. <http://cdiac.esd.ornl.gov/trends/co2/lawdome.html>, and for years after 1958 from Keeling's observations at Mauna Loa, <http://cdiac.esd.ornl.gov/ftp/maunaloa-co2/maunaloa.co2>. I thank Terry Tempest Williams for the idea of using this data as chapter leads. Her book, *Refuge,* similarly tracks the rise and fall of the Great Salt Lake.

Page 3   Several major environmental groups have co-published an excellent world map showing specific consequences of global warming. The map displays current *fingerprints* of global warming such as heat waves, sea level rise, melting glaciers, and polar warming; and *harbingers* of likely future impacts such as spreading disease, earlier

137

spring arrival, plant and animal range shifts, coral reef bleaching, droughts, fires, heavy snowfalls, and flooding. The map is accessible at <www.climatehotmap.org>. The report referred to in the text is by the National Assessment Synthesis Team (2000), <http://www.nacc. usgcrp.govl>.

Chapter 1 Winds of Change

Page 10   I encourage you to explore the Web sites of Working Assets, Redefining Progress, and the Corporation for Enterprise Development. Their respective addresses are <www.workingassets.com>, <www.rprogress. org>, and <www.cfed.org>.

Chapter 2. The Sky Is Filling!

Page 14   Because of nighttime light pollution, the Milky Way is invisible to 70 percent of Americans (*The Economist,* Sept. 9, 2000, p. 99).

Page 15   Zeus was the Greek god of the sky. In Greek mythology, Prometheus stole fire from the sky and gave it to humans. Zeus got angry and condemned Prometheus to eternal torture. The Greeks saw Prometheus as a hero, but with hindsight, it may be Zeus who was the wiser god. The fire Prometheus stole wasn't the right fire; because of it humans built an economy that harmed the earth. What we need now is a new Prometheus, one who cooperates with the gods to harness the sun's clean energy.

Page 18   My favorite books about the filling of the sky are Al Gore's *Earth in the Balance,* Bill McKibben's *The End of Nature,* and Richard Somerville's *The Forgiving Air.* The best account of Thomas Midgely's ill-fated inventions is in *Between Earth and Sky,* by Seth Cagin and Philip Dray.

Page 22   Weather-related losses reached $92 billion worldwide in 1998, according to the Munich Reinsurance Company. This topped the previous high of $60 billion, set in 1996, and exceeded the entire amount of weather-related losses during the 1980s. The El Niño and La Niña temperature shifts in the Pacific Ocean had a lot to do with the 1990s' tempestuous weather. Whether these oceanic changes are increasing in frequency and intensity as a result of global warming is a question that's being studied. See Brown et al., *Vital Signs 1999,* p. 74.

Page 24   For an exhaustive discussion of tipping points, see Malcolm Gladwell's *The Tipping Point: How Little Things Can Make a Big Difference* (2000).

Page 26   I'm indebted to economist Herman Daly for the idea of applying the Plimsoll line to environmental thresholds. Daly has written: "The major task of environmental macroeconomics is to design an economic institution analogous to the Plimsoll line—to keep the weight, the absolute scale, of the economy from sinking our biospheric ark." (*Beyond Growth*, p. 50).

Page 26   The precautionary principle emerged in the 1970s as a response to the environmental and health impacts of industrial growth. It's now a fundamental principle of German law.

Page 27   The IPCC's *Second Assessment Synthesis of Scientific-Technical Information* (1995) said a number of things. First: "Stabilization of the concentration of carbon dioxide at its present level could only be achieved through an immediate reduction in its emissions of 50–70% and further reductions thereafter." This, the panel deemed impossible. Second: "If the atmospheric concentration [of carbon dioxide] is to remain below 550 ppmv [twice the pre-industrial rate], the future global annual average emissions cannot, during the next century, exceed the current global average, and would have to be much lower before and beyond the end of the next century." <www.ipcc.ch/pub/sarsyn.htm>.

Page 30   "The existence of an area of free land, its continuous recession, and the advance of American settlement westward, explain American development," Turner wrote in 1893. Three years earlier, the U.S. Census Bureau had announced the closing of the frontier and the effective end of free land.

Chapter 3. Selling the Sky

Page 33   Frank Popoff's quote can be found in *Chemical and Engineering News*, January 11, 1993. Chief Seattle's quote appeared in *The Irish Press*, June 4, 1976. Apparently, they're not the Chief's actual words, but an embellished version written by Ted Perry of Middlebury College.

Page 35   Garrett Hardin also missed the point that it's unbridled market forces *around* the commons that bring forth the destructive behavior he laments. Years later, Hardin admitted he was wrong in condemning common ownership as inherently self-destructive.

Page 36 To extend the parking metaphor, imagine you're parking your car in that public garage, or simply on Main Street. There's a meter, and you drop 25 cents into it. "That's fair," you think, "because parking spaces on public streets are a scarce—and valuable—common asset. We don't want people just leaving their cars there, so we charge by the hour and penalize users if they don't pay."

Parking carbon dioxide in the sky (the average carbon dioxide molecule lingers 100 years there) is like parking your car on a public street or garage, so why shouldn't we set up a metering system up there? Instead of minutes of car parking, we'd charge for years of carbon dioxide parking. And our prices—compared to what it costs to park a car in New York City—would be incredibly cheap: only $1 a year to park a ton of carbon in the sky (the equivalent of a $100/ton price for a carbon emission permit). Such a deal!

Page 36 I've been trying to discover the inventor of cap-and-trade systems; in my opinion, this person (or persons) deserves a Nobel prize. The leading candidates, I'm told, are Tom Crocker and John Dales, both obscure economics professors.

In 1966, Crocker published an article called "The Structuring of Atmospheric Pollution Control Systems," in which he outlined a cap-and-trade system for reducing air pollution. Independently, Dales published an article in 1968 on water pollution in which he wrote: "Let it [the government] therefore issue *x* pollution rights and put them up for sale simultaneously passing a law that everyone who discharges one equivalent ton of waste during a year must hold one pollution right throughout the year. Since *x* is less than the number of equivalent tons of waste being discharged at present, the rights will command a positive price. The virtues of the market mechanism are that no person, or agency, has to set the price; it is set by the competition among buyers and sellers of rights. All that is required to make the market work is the inflexible resolve of the government not to change the rights issue during the interval, and to enforce rigidly the requirement that a ton-year of waste discharge must be paid for by the holding of one pollution right for the year."

However, University of California economics professor Richard Norgaard advises, "Don't give economists too much credit. City planning
departments for decades had cap-and-trade schemes on building
heights to facilitate an interesting skyline and sunlight hitting the
streets." In effect, these were sky usage rights trading systems.
    A good description of the sulfur cap-and-trade system can be found
at the Environmental Protection Agency's acid rain Web site, <www.
epa.gov/acidrain/trading.html.>

Page 37   Environmental justice advocates have criticized cap-and-trade systems
on the grounds that they result in pollution being shifted to low-
income and minority communities. However, such criticism applies
only to local pollutants. It doesn't apply to carbon, which is nontoxic,
disperses freely in the air, and causes global rather than local damage.

Page 37   In 1916, Sarnoff, then a contracts manager at the Marconi Company, sent a memo to his boss suggesting the use of radio for entertainment. "I have in mind a plan of development which would
make radio a household utility in the same sense as the piano or
phonograph. The receiver can be designed in the form of a simple
'Radio Music Box' . . . [which] can be placed in the parlor or living
room." Three years later he became general manager of the Radio
Corporation of America and made his vision a reality.

Page 38   The value of the spectrum has, if anything, increased since the
1995 giveaway, thanks to the proliferation of wireless phones,
pagers, and Internet access devices. "There is a severe spectrum
shortage," says Peter Cramton, an economics professor at the University of Maryland. "Recent auctions of frequencies in Britain
and Germany fetched tens of billions of dollars more than
expected; soon the United States will recapture and auction previously allocated spectrum." "Spectrum has become the most valuable asset of this new economy," the *New York Times* reported, "as
important as oil and coal were in the Industrial Revolution."
Stephen Labaton, "Clinton Orders a New Auction of the Airwaves," *New York Times,* Oct. 14, 2000.

Page 39   Costanza's $33 trillion estimate of the value of ecosystem services has
been challenged by several economists who say his methodologies
were flawed. Costanza has replied: "This is an order of magnitude

study, a first cut. Probably most economists would have guessed 1 percent of GNP or less. They're in the wrong order of magnitude. Therefore this issue requires a lot more attention." One of his co-authors, Stephen Farber, added: "I don't place a lot of credibility on the $33 trillion figure. But if we tried to satisfy [our critics], dooms-day would be past before we got any useful knowledge out there."

Page 41   The less-is-more magic of scarcity rent will work for a while, but not forever. At some point, low-carbon or no-carbon energy technologies will be widely deployed, and the demand for carbon permits will become elastic. At that point, less will become less, and Sky Trust rev-enue will shrink as it sells fewer carbon permits. No one, of course, knows when we'll hit this point, though it's safe to say that by the time we do, we'll have broken our current addiction to fossil fuels. Divi-dends from carbon permit revenue will also go down at that point, but by then they may be supplemented by dividends from other common assets.

Page 42   Ecological economists like Herman Daly have emphasized the superi-ority of resource usage caps over Pigovian taxes, and of upstream rather than downstream permit systems. Upstream caps (or quotas, as Daly calls them) "definitively limit aggregate throughput," whereas "taxes exert only an indirect and very uncertain limit." Taxes "intervene at the wrong end with the wrong policy tool," Daly wrote in *Economics, Ecology, Ethics* (1980).

Page 43   The most progressive ways to offset a carbon tax would be to expand the refundable Earned Income Tax Credit or lower the payroll tax. Lowering the payroll tax would, however, pry open the Pandora's box of Social Security. There's also the question of whose payroll taxes you'd cut. If you cut the employers' portion, you'd give a windfall to businesses and their owners. Cutting the workers' portion would be more progressive. But even then, you'd only offset the carbon taxes paid by active workers. Retired people, stay-at-home parents, unem-ployed workers, students, disabled people, and children—which is to say, a majority of the population—would get no benefits. Only a per capita distribution would cover everyone.

Page 44   Coase wrote about Pigovian taxes: "The proposal to solve the smoke-pollution and similar problems by the use of taxes bristles with diffi-culties: the problem of calculation, the difference between average and marginal damage, the interrelations between the damage suffered on different properties, etc." Further: "As it is not proposed that the proceeds of the tax should be paid to those suffering the damage, this solution is not the same as that which would force a business to pay compensation to those damaged by its actions" ("The Problem of Social Cost," 1960).

Chapter 4. Who Owns the Sky?

Page 47   On Roman law, see the Institutes of Justinian, especially the section on the classification of "things" <www.fordham.edu/halsall/basis/535institutes.html>. The seminal work on the public trust doctrine is Joseph L. Sax's 1970 *Michigan Law Review* article. Also helpful is Harry R. Bader's "Antaeus and the Public Trust Doctrine." According to the latter, courts have identified hunting, fishing, boating, swimming, retaining open space, preserving wildlife habitat, maintaining aesthetic beauty, and preserving ecological integrity as legitimate public expectations protected by the public trust doctrine.

On the question of global equity, which I have avoided in this book, the reader may want to explore the Web site of the London-based Global Commons Institute. GCI is promoting the concept of "contract and converge" as a way to resolve the dispute between rich and poor countries about how to share the global atmosphere. Under "contract and converge," the per capita emissions of the rich and poor countries would converge to equality over, say, fifty years. During this time, *total* global emissions would contract. But because poor countries' per capita emissions are far below the rich countries' (the average American emits six times as much carbon dioxide as the average Chinese person), the poor countries' emissions would actually rise at first. Though considered a radical idea just a few years ago, "contract and converge" is slowly gaining acceptance. <www.gci.org.uk>

The World Council of Churches also takes a strong position in favor of global equity. It states, "The atmosphere is a global commons. It envelops the Earth, nurturing and protecting life. It is part of God's creation. It is to be shared by everyone, today and in the future." The WCC recommends a Global Atmospheric Commons Model based on a per capita allocation of global emissions rights, as opposed to an allocation based on historical emissions. (Statement adopted in Saskatoon, Canada, May 14, 2000.)

Page 51   The Supreme Court case that equalized Alaska's dividends was *Zobel v. Williams,* 457 U.S. 55 (1982). The decision, written by Chief Justice Burger, declared: "When a state distributes benefits unequally, the distinctions it makes are subject to scrutiny under the Equal Protection Clause of the Fourteenth Amendment. Generally, a law will survive that scrutiny if the distinction it makes rationally furthers a legitimate state purpose . . . Alaska has shown no valid state interests that are rationally served by the distinctions it makes between citizens who established residence before 1959 and those who have become residents since then . . . Alaska's reasoning could . . . permit the states to divide citizens into expanding numbers of permanent classes. Such a result would be clearly impermissible." The only dissenter was Justice Rehnquist.

Chapter 5. How a Sky Trust Would Work

Page 64   The Sky Trust differs from the Permanent Fund in two other ways. First, its underlying asset, the carbon absorption capacity of the sky, is sustainable if properly managed, whereas Alaska's oil isn't. Second, the Sky Trust would have more control over the price of its asset than the Permanent Fund does. Oil prices are set on the world market, mostly by Saudi Arabia. The United States' price of carbon emission permits, by contrast, would depend on the quantity issued within the United States. The fewer permits issued, the higher their price. Thus, Sky Trust beneficiaries would gain from conservation of their asset, while Alaskans, in theory, gain from exploitation of theirs. (In fact, most of the income of the Alaska Permanent Fund now comes from investments rather than from oil. What really boosts Alaskans' dividends is a soaring stock market.)

Page 64   The numbers quoted on the distributional effect of the Sky Trust assume there's domestic carbon trading only. If international trading is permitted, U.S. firms could purchase emission rights from other countries at lower cost than they'd pay domestically. These externally acquired permits would allow them to emit within the United States and could actually result in an *increase* in U.S. emissions. Foreign permit purchases would also lower the amount of scarcity rent the Sky Trust would recycle. The distributional impact would be to reduce the gains of low-income households—in other words. to make the Sky Trust less progressive.

The coal industry will be hard hit by any policy that reduces carbon emissions. That's because coal dumps about twice as much carbon into the air per unit of energy as does natural gas, and about 1.5 times as much as oil. When carbon prices rise, coal burners (mostly utilities in the Midwest) will therefore start switching to natural gas.

Page 65 For a discussion of the Sky Trust's "safety valve," see Kopp et al. (1999).

Page 76 The most optimistic of the macroeconomic studies is the one by the Tellus Institute et. al. (1997). It found that by making cost-effective investments in energy conservation and renewable energy, the United States could cut carbon emissions to 10 percent below the 1990 level by 2010 while creating 770,000 new jobs.

Page 77 The statement by twenty-five hundred economists can be found at <www.rprogress.org/pubs/ecstat.html>

Chapter 6. Thought Experiments for Economists

Page 80 The idea that the marginal utility of stuff declines as wealth increases isn't novel. In 1738, mathematician Daniel Bernoulli observed that the satisfaction resulting from any small increase in wealth "will be inversely proportionate to the quantity of goods previously possessed" (cited in Bernstein, p. 5).

While it's true that externalities were smaller in the past, let's not forget that the death rate in cities like Manchester was much higher than in the countryside, and that England was almost completely deforested by the middle of the nineteenth century

Page 80 Galbraith, *The Affluent Society,* p. 4.

Page 84 Herman Daly's story about Larry Summers is recounted in *Beyond Growth,* pp. 6–7.

Page 86 Another peculiarly modern form of illth is losses caused by computer viruses. According to *Information Week,* some 50,000 U.S. firms are large enough to tally up the costs of software viruses. The bill to these firms for downtime, missed sales opportunities, and cleanup costs was $266 billion in 2000, or more than 3 percent of GDP! And this doesn't count the times company servers crashed for mysterious reasons of their own, with no help at all from hackers (a problem I'm personally familiar with). We can only hope the productivity *gains* from computer networks are greater than this.

Page 87   Another modern form of illth is stress. "Stress is a factor in over 70 percent of all doctor visits, according to the National Institute of Mental Health. 'Nearly every patient I see leads a life influenced in some way by inordinate levels of stress,' writes Dr. Richard Swenson of the University of Wisconsin Medical School in his book *Margin.* Stress is in large measure a product of the economy. It comes from the barrage of stimuli, the prolixity of choices, the pressures to perform and the multiplying claims upon our attention and time" (Rowe 1999).

Page 89   Luca Pacioli, an Italian mathematician who lived in Venice in the 1400s, invented double-entry bookkeeping as a way to help business people keep track of their transactions and make sense of their businesses. "If you cannot be a good accountant," Pacioli wrote, "you will grope your way forward like a blind man and may meet great losses." The accounting procedures in use today keep tabs not only of actual cash transactions, but also of fictitious transactions that give a more accurate picture of a business's health. The most common of these fictions is *depreciation.* Another is that mysterious item on corporate balance sheets called *goodwill.* The point for our purposes is that useful fictions are already part of everyday business. We should have no compunctions about inventing new ones if, like the old ones, they give us a better picture of reality.

Page 94   According to the Direct Marketing Association, Madison Avenue spent $285 billion in 1998 urging us to buy things. That doesn't include money spent by small local businesses. <www.the-dma.org>

Page 95   In a 1997 poll of eight-hundred households, conducted for the Center for a New American Dream, 33 percent indicated that between 25 and 50 percent of the things they buy are things they don't really need. A majority of respondents, 55 percent, said they'd be willing to reduce material possessions and earnings by "some" or "a lot" to gain time with family and to experience less stress. <www .newdream.org/newsletter/tradepay.html>

Page 95   Concerning surplus economies, Galbraith wrote in *The Affluent Society*: "If people who have always lived within nodding distance of poverty and privation become, by contrast, comparatively well-to-do, we must assume this will have a bearing on their wants and economic behavior, and hence on the ideas by which these are interpreted" (p. vi). And further: "Production for the sake of the goods produced is no longer very urgent. The significance of marginal increments (or decrements) in the supply of goods is slight" (p. 197).

Page 96   The desire for more time, as opposed to more money and stuff, isn't just a phenonenon of post-industrial affluence; it may represent something deeper. Max Weber, writing in 1904 about the origins of capitalism, observed that early capitalist employers had a hard time getting workers motivated. When they wanted higher production, they raised piece-rates. But, noted Weber, "a peculiar difficulty has been met with surprising frequency: raising the piece-rates has often had the result that not more but less has been accomplished in the same time, because the worker reacted to the increase not by increasing but by decreasing his amount of work . . . The opportunity of earning more was less attractive than that of working less." The implication is, we had to be *taught* to want more money and stuff.

Page 99   Regarding intergenerational transfers, there's also the matter of *when* inheritances are received. In the old days, when humans died young, children received their inheritances while in their twenties and thirties. Those were ages at which inheritances could be put to productive use—for buying land or a home, or starting a business. Nowadays, Americans don't die until their eighties, which means their kids are in their fifties and sixties when they take possession of the family jewels. These latter-day inheritances may sweeten retirement, but they're too late to capitalize the wealth-building years.

Chapter 7. The New Commons

Page 110   Here's a personal story about unearned capital gains. The house I bought in San Francisco in 1974 for $53,000 is now worth close to $1 million. What did I do to earn this gain? Beats me. The gain has almost nothing to do with me. It has a lot to do with silicon, the Internet, and those dot.commers thinking my neighborhood is hip. It's as if, every year for the past twenty-seven years, I'd been given a virtually tax-free $30,000 bonus to put in my retirement account—just for having bought a house for $10,000 down (with a 7 percent mortgage).

On the distribution of private assets: According to the lastest Federal Reserve Board survey of U.S. consumers, less than half of American workers held any stock at all, including through mutual funds and 401(k) plans.

Page 112 An auction of new road miles would require some differentiation between first roads in pristine areas and additional roads in built-up areas. The former cause more habitat loss than the latter, and should therefore be more restricted.

In 1999, the U.S. Forest Service imposed a road-building moratorium in order to reevaluate its management of 373,000 miles of roads in National Forests.

Page 114 Quietude is disappearing even inside National Parks. "Even at isolated parks, the sounds of civilization—the internal combustion engine, the car alarm, the jack hammer—intrude on the visitor's ear. Too often lost in the hubbub are the wind in the trees and the singing birds . . . Park Service officials are so concerned they're expected to ask all park superintendents to find ways to protect what's known as the soundscape, the blend of natural sounds unique to every park" (Tracy Watson, "A Scarcity of Silence," *USA Today,* Sept. 20, 2000).

According to *Real Simple* magazine, the ten largest U.S. telemarketing firms employ enough people and have enough technology to place 21 million calls a day (Hope Reeves, "Don't Just Hang Up," *Real Simple,* Sept. 2000).

Disclosure statement: As this is written, I co-chair the board of the Noise Pollution Clearinghouse. The mission of the organization is "to create more civil cities and more natural rural and wilderness areas by reducing noise pollution at the source." The organization helps citizens throughout the United States fight noise from airplanes, traffic, jet skis, leaf blowers, and other sources. It has an enormously helpful Web site <www.nonoise.org>.

I'm also on the board of the TV Turnoff Network, which encourages children and adults to watch less television. According to the

A. C. Nielsen Co., the average American watches three hours and forty-six minutes of TV each day. By the time an American child graduates high school, s/he'll have seen 360,000 TV ads. By age sixty-five, two million. Concerned? Visit <www.tvturnoff.org>.

Page 115   Ironically, if government were to enforce a Sabbath today, this would be called a "command and control" approach and denounced by free market conservatives.

Page 116   Memo to Alan Greenspan: Here's how changing the rate of *spectrum* use can fight inflation better than changing the rate of *money* use. Nowadays, when inflation threatens, you (i.e., the Fed) raise interest rates. That makes money more costly to businesses, so they slow down. Demand dampens, and prices fall. Unfortunately, there are side effects. When interest rates go up, innocent bystanders suffer. People with variable rate mortgages, car loans, or credit card balances get socked. People who were *hoping* to buy a home or car can't do it. Bankruptcies rise, workers are laid off. But now imagine a different scenario. When inflation threatens, the Quietude Trust lowers the quantity of advertising permitted. Demand dampens, and prices fall. And no one's mortgage payments go up. The inflation medicine is just as effective—and a lot less bitter.

Page 117   The total amount candidates spent on TV ads during 1996 was $2.5 billion. That's $2.5 billion paid to companies who received the airwaves for nothing. It's also a measure of the extent to which candidates must cater to business interests to pay for TV advertising.

Page 117   Concentration of airwave ownership may actually be decreasing at the moment. The early years of radio were dominated by three networks, one owned by CBS and two by NBC. The government forced NBC to divest one of its networks, which became ABC. Today, ABC, CBS, and Westwood One (which acquired NBC's radio holdings) have about 25 percent of the radio audience. Similarly, in television, ABC, CBS, and NBC had 90 percent of prime-time viewers in the early 1980s. Today, thanks to competition from new networks and cable, the Big Three's share has dropped to 50 percent (Noam, 1996). To me, that's still pretty concentrated, though.

Page 123 On future scarcities: Who owns the rain? That may be the next Zen koan to ponder if the oft-heard prediction of a twenty-first-century water shortage comes to pass. According to the International Water Management Institute, 1.8 billion people will live in regions with absolute water scarcity by 2025. The United States overall has plenty of water, but many cities—especially in the arid West—don't. An assortment of watershed and acquifer trusts may become necessary, superceding, though not entirely displacing, existing water rights. The scarcity rent for water may then approach that of sky.

Another looming scarcity is the biosphere's nitrogen-absorbing capacity. Nitrogen is a basic building block of proteins. Though it makes up 79 percent of the atmosphere, it can't be used by plants unless it's converted ("fixed") by certain bacteria and algae into ammonium or nitrate compounds. Until recently, the amount of fixed nitrogren available to plants has been relatively small. However, in the past few decades, massive use of fertilizers has changed that. Now, human-made plant-usable nitrogen far exceeds nature's production. Plants can absorb some of this extra nitrogen, but not all—and excess nitrogen has serious consequences. It depletes the soil of other nutrients, contributes to smog, acid rain, ozone destruction, and global warming, and stimulates growth of algae. This latter process, called *eutrophication,* is a threat to fish, seabirds, and marine mammals in coastal waters (*World Resources 1998–1999,* pp. 179–181). What if we have to cut nitrogen use by 50 percent? Curbing our nitrogen habit may be almost as difficult as curbing our carbon habit. If a cap-and-trade system is used, the scarcity rent for nitrogren absorption capacity could be substantial.

How large (relative to GDP) could the new commons, as a sum of many common asset trusts, grow? The Sky Trust alone, with the single asset of carbon absorption capacity, could have revenue in the range of 3 percent of GDP. The contributions of other trusts would depend on asset definitions and the usage limits set. One quick and very dirty way to estimate the potential size of the new commons is to use Redefining Progress's estimates of illth. If externalities are roughly half of GDP, and we're bold enough to "assetize" half of them, then the common sector could, in theory, grow to 25 percent of GDP. I'd be thrilled if it grew to 10 percent, which is the current scale of social insurance.

Chapter 8. Capitalism 2.0

Page 130 Keynes did have some thoughts about how to get from greed to gentility. In a 1925 essay, he called for an end to the "hereditary principle in the transmission of wealth," which is "not in the least characteristic of [capitalism], but which it took over from the social system of Feudalism which preceded it." A year later he wrote: "Our task must be to decentralize and devolve wherever we can, and in particular to establish semi-independent corporations and organs of administration to which duties of government, new and old, will be entrusted—without, however, impairing the democratic principle" (*Essays in Persuasion*, 1930). I like both suggestions.

Page 131 The international battle for atmospheric scarcity rent is already raging. In addition to the conflict between developing nations (who favor a per capita allocation of the global atmosphere) and developed nations (who favor an allocation based on historic use), there's a hard-nosed battle between oil exporting and oil consuming countries. Thus, at the September 2000 meeting of OPEC, the oil exporting cartel announced that it would increase production only if consuming nations lowered their fuel taxes. "We are willing to raise production to keep prices stable," said Iranian president Mohammed Khatami, "but we are concerned about high taxes, and we ask for measures to rectify this." (Collier, *San Francisco Chronicle*, Sept. 28, 2000.) Translation: There's only so much scarcity rent to go around. Right now, consuming nations' governments (especially in Europe) capture a good chunk of that rent through taxes. The OPEC nations would like to collect a greater share themselves and want to gain that greater share at the expense of the consuming countries' governments (which means, ultimately, at the expense of their social welfare programs). However this battle turns out, it clearly compounds the difficulty Western governments have in raising oil or carbon taxes. This in turn strengthens the case for market-based mechanisms such as the Sky Trust.

Bibliography

The number of books and articles that have been written about climate change, management of the commons, and economic theory in general, is staggering. I list only those that are drawn upon in the text, or that have significantly contributed to my thinking.

Books

Ackerman, Bruce, and Anne Alstott, *The Stakeholder Society,* Yale University Press, New Haven: 1999.

Agarwal, Anil, Sunita Narain, and Anju Sharma, *Green Politics: Global Environmental Negotiations,* Centre for Science and the Environment, New Delhi: 1999.

Ashworth, William, *The Economy of Nature: Rethinking the Connections Between Ecology and Economics,* Houghton Mifflin, Boston: 1995.

Athanasiou, Tom, *Divided Planet: The Ecology of Rich and Poor,* Little, Brown & Co., Boston: 1996.

Baden, John A., and Douglass S. Noonan, editors, *Managing the Commons,* Indiana University Press, Bloomington: 1998.

Bernstein, Peter L., *Against the Gods: The Remarkable Story of Risk,* John Wiley & Sons, New York: 1996.

Brown, Lester, Michael Renner, and Brian Halweil, *Vital Signs 1999: The Environmental Trends That Are Shaping Our Future,* Worldwatch Institute, W. W. Norton, New York: 1999.

Buck, Susan J. *The Global Commons,* Island Press, Washington, D.C.: 1998.

Cagin, Seth, and Philip Dray, *Between Earth and Sky: How CFCs Changed Our World and Endangered the Ozone Layer,* Pantheon Books, New York: 1993.

Capra, Fritjof, *The Web of Life,* Doubleday, New York: 1996.

Carson, Rachel, *Silent Spring,* Houghton Mifflin, Boston: 1962.

Cleveland, Harlan, *The Global Commons: Policy for the Planet,* University Press of America, Lanham MD: 1990.

Coase, R. H., *Essays on Economics and Economists,* University of Chicago Press, Chicago: 1994.

Daily, Gretchen, editor, *Nature's Services: Societal Dependence on Natural Ecosystems,* Island Press, Washington, D.C.: 1997. <www.islandpress.com/ecocompass/nature/nsec.html>

Dales, J. H., *Pollution, Property and Prices,* University of Toronto Press, Toronto: 1968.

Daly, Herman, *Beyond Growth,* W. H. Freeman & Co., San Francisco: 1997.

Daly, Herman, editor, *Economics, Ecology, Ethics: Essays Toward a Steady-State Economy,* W. H. Freeman & Co., San Francisco: 1980.

Daly, Herman, and John B. Cobb Jr., *For the Common Good,* Beacon Press, Boston: 1989.

Demillo, Rob, *How Weather Works,* Ziff-Davis Press, Emeryville: 1994.

Dorfman, Robert, and Nancy S. Dorfman, editors, *Economics of the Environment,* W. W. Norton, New York: 1977.

The Ecologist, *Whose Common Future? Reclaiming the Commons,* New Society Publishers, Philadelphia: 1993.

Ehrlich, Paul R., *The Population Bomb,* Ballantine, New York: 1968.

Firor, John, *The Changing Atmosphere,* Yale University Press, New Haven: 1990.

Galbraith, John Kenneth, *The Affluent Society,* Houghton Mifflin, Boston: 1958.

Gates, Jeff, *Democracy At Risk,* Perseus Publishers, Cambridge: 2000.

Geisler, Charles, and Gail Daneker, editors, *Property and Values: Alternatives to Public and Private Ownership,* Island Press, Washington, D.C.: 2000.

Gelbspan, Ross, *The Heat Is On: The Climate Crisis, The Cover-Up, The Prescription,* Addison-Wesley, Reading: 1997.

George, Henry, *Progress and Poverty,* Robert Schalkenbach Foundation, New York: 1966. First published in 1880.

Gladwell, Malcolm, *The Tipping Point: How Little Things Can Make a Big Difference,* Little, Brown & Co., Boston: 2000.

Goodenough, Ursula, *The Sacred Depths of Nature,* Oxford University Press, Oxford: 1998.

Gore, Al, *Earth in the Balance,* Houghton Mifflin, Boston: 1992.

Gray, Rob, Jan Bebbington, and Diane Walters, *Accounting for the Environment,* Markus Wiener, Princeton: 1993.

Haddad, Brent M., *Rivers of Gold: Designing Markets to Allocate Water in California,* Island Press, Washington, D.C.: 2000.

Hammond, Jay, *Tales of Alaska's Bush Rat Governor,* Epicenter Press, Fairbanks: 1996.

Hawken, Paul, *The Ecology of Commerce,* HarperCollins, New York: 1993.

Hawken, Paul, Amory Lovins, and L. Hunter Lovins, *Natural Capitalism: Creating the Next Industrial Revolution,* Little Brown & Co., Boston: 1999.

Heilbroner, Robert, *The Worldly Philosophers,* Touchstone Books, New York: 1987.

———, *21st Century Capitalism,* W. W. Norton, New York: 1993.

Hertsgaard, Mark, *Earth Odyssey,* Broadway Books, New York: 1998.

Hyde, Lewis, *The Gift: Imagination and the Erotic Life of Property,* Vintage, New York: 1979.

Keynes, John Maynard, *Essays in Persuasion,* Norton, New York: 1963. First published in 1930.

———, *The General Theory of Employment, Interest and Money,* Harcourt Brace, New York: 1989. First published in 1936.

Kuttner, Robert, *Everything for Sale: The Virtues and Limits of Markets,* Knopf, New York: 1997.

Lasn, Kalle, *Culture Jam: The Uncooling of America,* William Morrow, New York: 1999.

Levine, Robert, *A Geography of Time,* Basic Books, New York: 1997.

Linden, Eugene, *The Future in Plain Sight: Nine Clues to the Coming Instability,* Simon & Schuster, New York: 1998.

Lovelock, James E., *Gaia: A New Look at Life on Earth*, Oxford University Press, Oxford: 1979.

————, *Healing Gaia: Practical Medicine for the Planet*, Crown Publishers, New York: 1991.

Lovins, Amory, *Soft Energy Paths*, Harper, New York: 1977.

Malthus, Thomas Robert, *An Essay on the Principle of Population*, Penguin USA, New York: 1985. First published in 1798.

Maslow, Abraham, *Toward a Psychology of Being*, John Wiley & Sons, New York: 1998. First published in 1968.

Mayer, Carl J., and George A. Riley, *Public Domain, Private Domain: A History of Public Mineral Policy in America*, Sierra Club Books, San Francisco: 1985.

Maunder, W. J., *The Value of Weather*, Methuen & Co., London: 1970.

McKibben, Bill, *The End of Nature*, Random House, New York: 1989.

Meadows, Donella H., et al., *The Limits to Growth*, Universe Books, New York: 1972.

Meadows, Donella H., Dennis L. Meadows, and Jørgen Randers, *Beyond the Limits*, Chelsea Green Press, White River Junction VT: 1992.

Mishan, E. J., *The Economic Growth Debate*, George Allen & Unwin, London: 1977.

Nordhaus, William D., *Managing the Global Commons: The Economics of Change*, MIT Press, Cambridge: 1994.

Ostrom, Elinor, *Governing the Commons*, Cambridge University Press, New York: 1990.

Pigou, Arthur C., *The Economics of Welfare*, Macmillan, London: 1920.

Ponting, Clive, *A Green History of the World: The Environment and the Collapse of Great Civilizations*, St. Martin's Press, New York: 1992.

Revkin, Andrew, *Global Warming: Understanding the Forecast*, Abbeville Press, New York: 1992.

Ricardo, David, *On the Principles of Political Economy and Taxation*, John Murray, London: 1817. <www.socsci.mcmaster.ca/~econ/ugcm/3ll3/ricardo/prin/prin1.txt>

Roodman, David Malin, *The Natural Wealth of Nations*, W. W. Norton, New York: 1998.

Rothschild, Michael, *Bionomics: The Inevitability of Capitalism*, Henry Holt, New York: 1990.

Ruskin, John, *Unto This Last*, Penguin USA, New York: 1986. First published in 1860.

Russell, Jeffrey Burton, *A History of Heaven*, Princeton University Press, Princeton: 1997.

Schafer, R. Murray, *The Soundscape*, Destiny Books, Rochester VT: 1977.

Scherf, Judith, editor, *The Piracy of America: Profiteering in the Public Domain*, Clarity Press, Atlanta: 1999.

Schneider, Steven H., *Laboratory Earth*, Basic Books, New York: 1998.

Schor, Juliet B., *The Overworked American*, Basic Books, New York: 1993.

Schumacher, E. F., *Small Is Beautiful: Economics as if People Mattered*, Harper & Row, New York: 1973.

Shanks, Bernard, *This Land Is Your Land*, Sierra Club Books, San Francisco: 1984.

Sherraden, Michael, *Assets and the Poor: A New American Welfare Policy*, M.E. Sharpe, Armonk NY: 1991.

Simon, Julian, *The Ultimate Resource*, Princeton University Press, Princeton: 1998.

Smith, Adam, *The Wealth of Nations*, Penguin Edition, London: 1982. First published in 1776.

Somerville, Richard C. J., *The Forgiving Air: Understanding Environmental Change*, University of California Press, Berkeley: 1996.

Steinberg, Theodore, *Slide Mountain: The Folly of Owning Nature*, University of California Press, Berkeley: 1995.

Suzuki, David, *The Sacred Balance: Rediscovering Our Place in Nature*, Prometheus Books, Amherst NY: 1998.

Tudge, Colin, *The Time Before History: 5 Million Years of Human Impact*, Simon & Schuster, New York: 1997.

Turner, Frederick Jackson, *The Frontier in American History*, Dover, Mineola NY: 1996. First published in 1893.

Volk, Tyler, *Gaia's Body: Toward a Physiology of the Earth*, Springer-Verlag, New York: 1998.

Weber, Max, *The Protestant Ethic and the Spirit of Capitalism*, Charles Scribner's Sons, New York: 1958. First published in 1904.

Wilson, E. O., *The Diversity of Life*, W. W. Norton, New York: 1993.

World Resources Institute, U.N. Environment Programme, U.N. Development Program and the World Bank, *World Resources 1998–99*, Oxford University Press, Oxford: 1998.

Articles, Reports, and Papers

If an article or paper is accessible on the Internet, I've given an address to find it. Bear in mind, however, that Internet addresses and contents change over time.

Anderson, Dean, and Michael Grubb, editors, *Controlling Carbon and Sulphur*, Royal Institute of International Affairs, London: 1997.

Andrews, Edmund L., "Airwaves Plan Is Called Give-away to Broadcasters," *N.Y. Times*, Oct. 28, 1995.

Arrhenius, Svante, "On the Influence of Carbonic Acid in the Air upon the Temperature on the Ground," *Philosophical Magazine* 41, 1896. <http://maple.lemoyne.edu/~giunta/Arrhenius.html>

Bader, Harry R., "Antaeus and the Public Trust Doctrine: A New Approach to Substantive Environmental Protection in the Common Law," 19 *Boston College of Environmental Affairs Law Review*, Boston: 1992.

Barlow, Maude, *Blue Gold: The Global Water Crisis and the Commodification of the World's Water Supply*, International Forum on Globalization, San Francisco: 1999.

Barnes, Peter, "Pie in the Sky," Corporation for Enterprise Development, *1997 Entrepreneurial Economy Review*, Washington, D.C.: 1998.

———, "The Pollution Dividend," *The American Prospect*, May/June 1999. <www.prospect.org/archives/44/44barnes.html>

———, "One Sky, Many Owners," *N.Y. Times*, May 11, 1997.

———, "Earned vs. Unearned Income," *The New Republic*, October 7, 1972.

———, "The Great American Land Grab," *The New Republic*, June 5, 1971.

Barrett, James, and J. Andrew Hoerner, *Making Green Policies Pay Off*, Economic Policy Institute, Washington, D.C.: April 2000.

Bennett, Ralph Kinney, "The Great Airwaves Giveaway," *Reader's Digest*, June 1996.

Boggs, R., "Samuel Plimsoll and the Load Line," <http://home.pacifier.com/~rboggs/plimsoll.html> (1996).

Boulding, Kenneth, "The Economics of the Coming Spaceship Earth," *Environmental Quality in a Growing Economy*, Johns Hopkins Press, Baltimore: 1966.

Britton, Douglas, "The Privatization of the American Fishery," 3 *Ocean and Coastal Law Journal* 217 (1997).

Brown, Paige, *Fair and Low-Cost Climate Protection*, Redefining Progress, San Francisco: 1999. <www.rprogress.org/pubs/publist.html>

Charles River Associates, *Economic Implications of the Adoption of Limits on Carbom Emissions from Industrialized Countries*, Charles River Associates, Washington, D.C.: 1997.

Coase, Ronald H., "The Federal Communications Commission," *The Journal of Law and Economics*, Vol. 2, 1–29. Chicago: 1959.

Coase, Ronald H., "The Problem of Social Cost," *The Journal of Law and Economics*, Vol. 3, 1–44. Chicago: 1960.

Cobb, Clifford, Ted Halstead, and Jonathan Rowe, "If the GDP Is Up, Why Is America Down?", *Atlantic Monthly*, October 1995. <www.theatlantic.com/politics/ecbig/gdp.htm>

Cobb, Clifford, Gary Sue Goodman, and Mathis Wackernagel, *Why Bigger Isn't Better: The Genuine Progress Indicator—1999 Update*, Redefining Progress, San Francisco: 1999. <www.rprogress.org/pubs/gpi1999/gpi19999.html>

Common Cause, "Channeling Influence: The Broadcast Lobby & The $70 Billion Free Ride," April 1997. <www.commoncause.org/publications/040297rpt.htm>

Congressional Budget Office, *Where Do We Go From Here? The FCC Auctions and the Future of Radio Spectrum Management*, Washington, D.C.: 1997. <www.cbo.gov>

———, *Who Gains and Who Pays Under Carbon Allowance Trading?* Congressional Budget Office, Washington, D.C.: 2000. <www.cbo.gov>

Costanza, Robert, Ralph d'Arge, Rudolf de Groot, Stephen Farber, Monica Grasso, Bruce Hannon, Karin Limburg, Shahid Naeem, Robert V. O. O'Neill, Jose Pareulo, Robert G. Raskin, Paul Sutton, and Marjan van den Belt, "The Value of the World's Ecosystem Services and Natural Capital," *Nature*, May 12, 1997.

Cramton, Peter, and Suzi Kerr, "Tradable Carbon Allowance Auctions: How and Why to Auction," Center for Clean Air Policy, Washington, D.C.: March 1998. <www.ccap.org/m-pub.htm>

Dales, J. H., "Land, Water and Ownership," *Canadian Journal of Economics,* November 1968. Reprinted in Dorfman (1977), pp. 229–251.

Driesen, David M., "Free Lunch or Cheap Fix: The Emissions Trading Idea and the Climate Change Convention," *Boston College Environmental Affairs Law Review,* Boston: 1998

Dudek, Daniel J., *Emissions Budgets: Creating Rewards, Lowering Costs and Ensuring Results,* paper presented at the Climate Change Analysis Workshop, June 6, 1996, in Springfield VA, Environmental Defense Fund, New York: 1996.

Ellerman, A. Denny. "Obstacles to Global CO_2 Trading: A Familiar Problem," Massachusetts Institute of Technology, Joint Program on the Science and Policy of Global Change, Report #42, Nov. 1998. <http://web.mit.edu/globalchange/www/rpt42.html>

Energy Information Administration, *Impacts of the Kyoto Protocol on U.S. Energy Markets and Economic Activity,* Washington, D.C.: Oct. 1998. <www.eia.doe.gov/oiaf/kyoto/kyotorpt.html>

———, *Analysis of the Impacts of an Early Start for Compliance with the Kyoto Protocol,* Washington, D.C.: July 1999. <www.eia.doe.gov/oiaf/kyoto3/kyoto3rpt.html>

Federal Reserve Board, "Recent Changes in U.S. Family Finances: Results from the 1998 Survey of Consumer Finances," *Federal Reserve Bulletin,* Washington, D.C.: January 2000. <www.federalreserve.gov/pubs/oss/oss2/98/bull0100.pdf>

Forman, Richard T. T., "Estimate of the Area Affected Ecologically by the Road System in the United States," *Conservation Biology,* February 2000.

H. John Heinz Center for Science, Economics and the Environment, *Designs for Domestic Carbon Emissions Trading,* Washington, D.C.: 1998. <www.heinzctr.org/programs/gcfinal.pdf>

Hamond, Jeff, Stephen DeCanio, Peggy Duxbury, Alan Sanstad, and Christopher H. Stinson, *Tax Waste, Not Work,* Redefining Progress, San Francisco: 1997. <www.rprogress.org/pubs/twnw/twnw contents.html>

Hamond, Jeff, Hardy Merriman, and Gary Wolff, *Equity and Distributional Issues in the Design of Environmental Tax Reform,* Redefining Progress, San Francisco: 1999. <www.rprogress.org/pubs/publist.html>

Hardin, Garrett, "The Tragedy of the Commons," *Science* 162(1968):1243–1248. <http://dieoff.org/page95.htm.>

Hargrave, Tim, "U.S. Carbon Emissions Trading: Description of an Upstream Approach," Center for Clean Air Policy, Washington DC: March 1998. <www.ccap.org/m-pub.htm>

Havens, John, and Paul Schervish, "Millionaires and the Millennium: New Estimates of the Forthcoming Wealth Transfer and the Prospects for a Golden Age of Philanthropy," Social Welfare Research Institute, Boston College, Chestnut Hill MA: 1999. <www.bc.edu/bc_org/avp/gsas/swri/m&m.html>

Hulme, George V., "It's Time to Clamp Down: Attacks and Other Breaches Continue to Exact a Huge Toll," *Information Week,* July 10, 2000. <www.informationweek.com/794/security.htm>

Intergovernmental Panel on Climate Change (IPCC), *The Science of Climate Change: Summary for Policymakers,* Cambridge University Press, Cambridge: 1996. <http://www.ipcc.ch/pub/sarsum1.htm>

Interlaboratory Working Group on Energy-Efficient and Low-Carbon Technologies, *Scenarios of U.S. Carbon Reductions: Potential Impacts of Energy-Efficient and Low Carbon Technologies by 2010 and Beyond,* Oak Ridge National Laboratory, Lawrence Berkeley National Laboratory, Pacific Northwest National Laboratory, National Renewable Energy Laboratory, and Argonne National Laboratory: September1997.<www.ornl.gov/ORNL/Energy_Eff/labweb.htm>

Knize, Perri, "The Mismanagement of the National Forests," *Atlantic Monthly,* October 1991.

Kopp, Raymond, Richard Morgenstern, William Pizer, and Michael Toman, "A Proposal for Credible Early Action in U.S. Climate Policy," Resources for the Future, Washington, D.C.: Feb. 1999. <http://www.weathervane.rff.org/features/feature060.html>

Lewyn, Mark, "The Great Airwave Robbery," *Wired,* March 1996.

Liesman, Steven, and Jacob M. Schlesinger, "The Price of Oil Has Doubled This Year; So Where's the Recession?" *Wall Street Journal,* Dec. 15, 1999.

Metcalf, Gilbert E.,"A Distributional Analysis of An Environmental Tax Shift," National Bureau of Economic Research, Cambridge: 1998. <http://papers.nber.org/papers/W6546>

Miller, Bill, "Judge Orders Overhaul of Indian Trust Fund," *The Washington*

Post, Dec. 21, 1999. <www.washingtonpost.com/wpdyn/articles/A22093-1999Dec21.html>

National Assessment Synthesis Team, U.S. Global Change Research Program, *Climate Change Impacts on the United States,* Washington, D.C.: 2000. <http://www.nacc.usgcrp.gov/>

Noam, Eli M., *Media Concentration in the United States: Industry Trends and Regulatory Responses,* Virtual Institute of Information, Columbia University Business School, New York: 1996. <www.vii.org/papers/medconc.htm>

Ostrom, Elinor, "Revisiting the Commons: Local Lessons, Global Challenges," *Science* 284(1999):278–282.

Poterba, James M., "Is the Gasoline Tax Regressive?" In *Tax Policy and the Economy,* edited by David Bradford. MIT Press, Cambridge: 1991.

Probyn, Christopher, and Will Goetz, *Macroeconomic Impacts of Greenhouse Gas Control Policies,* presentation at the Climate Change Analysis Workshop, June 6, 1996, in Springfield VA, DRI/McGraw-Hill, Lexington MA: 1996.

Repetto, Robert, and Duncan Austin, *The Costs of Climate Protection: A Guide for the Perplexed.* World Resources Institute, Washington, D.C.: 1997.

Rowe, Jonathan, "The GDP Myth," *The Washington Monthly,* March 1999. <www.washingtonmonthly.com/features/1999/9903.rowe.growth.html>

Sachs, Wolfgang, "Rich in Goods, but Poor in Time," *Resurgence,* September/October 1999. <www.gn.apc.org/resurgence/issues/sachs196.htm>

Sax, Joseph L., "The Public Trust Doctrine in Natural Resource Law: Effective Judicial Intervention," 68 *Michigan Law Review,* Ann Arbor: 1970.

Schafer, R. Murray, *The Book of Noise,* Arcana Editions, Indian River, Ontario: 1998.

Seckler, David, David Molden, and Randolph Barker, *Water Scarcity in the Twenty-First Century,*" International Water Management Institute, Colombo: 1999. <www.cgiar.org/iwmi/index.htm>

Tellus Institute, Alliance to Save Energy, the American Council for an Energy-Efficient Economy, the Natural Resources Defense Council and the Union of Concerned Scientists, *Energy Innovations: A Prosperous Path to a Clean Environment,* Washington DC: 1997. <www.tellus.org/ei/index.html>

Torres, Gerald, unpublished legal memo, Corporation for Enterprise Development, Washington, D.C.: 1999. The question addressed in the memo is who owns currently unassigned natural resources.

Trombulak, Stephen C., and Christopher A. Frissell, "Review of Ecological Effects of Roads on Terrestrial and Aquatic Communities," *Conservation Biology,* February 2000.

United Nations, Framework Convention on Climate Change, adopted in Rio de Janeiro, May 9, 1992. <www.unfccc.org/resource/conv/conv.html>

Warsh, David, "Coase Wins Nobel," *Boston Globe,* Oct. 16, 1991; and "When the Revolution Was a Party: How Privatization Was Invented in the 1960s," *Boston Globe,* Oct. 20, 1991.

Watt, Helen Payne, *Common Assets: Asserting Rights to Our Shared Inheritance,* Corporation for Enterprise Development, Washington, D.C.: 2000.

WEFA, Inc., *Global Warming: The High Costs of the Kyoto Protocol,* Eddystone PA: 1998.

Weyant, John P., and Jennifer N. Hill, "Introduction and Overview," and Mac-Cracken, Christopher N., James A. Edmonds, Son H. Kim, and Ronald D. Sands, "The Economics of the Kyoto Protocol," *The Energy Journal, Special Issue: The Costs of the Kyoto Protocol: A Multi-Model Evaluation,* 1999.

Wolff, Edward N., "Recent Trends in Wealth Ownership," a paper for the conference on "Benefits and Mechanisms for Spreading Asset Ownership in the United States," New York University, New York: December 1998.

———, "How the Pie Is Sliced: America's Growing Concentration of Wealth," *The American Prospect,* Summer 1995. <www.prospect.org/archives/22/22wolf.html>

———, *Top Heavy: A Study of Increased Inequality of Wealth in America,* Twentieth Century Fund, New York: 1995.

World Council of Churches, *The Earth's Atmosphere: Responsible Caring and Equitable Sharing for a Global Commons,* Statement adopted in Saskatoon, Canada, May 14, 2000.

Index

Acid rain, 19–20, 36
Acquisition of stuff as path to
    happiness, 94
Advertising, 37, 114–16
Agriculture, 111
Airlines, 76
Alaska-style citizen ownership,
    50–53, 64, 127–29
America as a main polluter, 46
America the Beautiful, 23
Animal husbandry, 111
Antarctica, 20–22
Arrhenius, Svante, 18, 20
Asset, making the sky into an, 41.
    See also Commons, the new
Assetization, 107
Assets, private vs. common, 99–100,
    102
Asteroids, the sky shielding us from,
    16
Atmosphere as the most important
    part of biosphere, 14. *See also*
    Sky, the
Automobiles, 18–19

Babbitt, Bruce, 54

Baby Boomers, 98–99
Bates, Katherine L., 1, 22–23
Bateson, Gregory, 89
Bentham, Jeremy, 93
Benz, Karl, 18
Beyond the Limits, 84
Billboards, 114, 115–16
Biodiversity, 110–13
Blake, William, xi
Blizzards, 22
Borrowing, 90
Boulding, Kenneth, 22
Boundaries, 11, 83
Breslow, Marc, 64
Broadcast spectrum, 2, 17, 37–39,
    117

Cap-and-trade systems, 35–37, 62.
    See also Sky Trust
Capital gains, 110
Capitalism:
    citizen-shareholders, 127–29
    code, installing a new economic,
        131
    economists, thought experiments
        for, 97–98

Capitalism (*continued*)
  Faustian deal millennial capitalism
    offers, 130
  future of, 131–32
  incentives driving, 129
  Keynes, John M., 129–30
  operating system of, 126
  Smith, Adam, 125
  systemic change, 130–31
  trust funds, 131
  twenty-first-century upgrade of,
    100–103, 126
  See also Commons, the new;
    Selling the sky
Carbon dioxide:
  America placing most of the excess
    in the sky, 46
  Antarctica, 20–21
  Arrhenius, Svante, 18
  disasters, natural, 22
  fossil fuel combustion, inescapable
    by-product of, 4
  Intergovernmental Panel on
    Climate Change, 27–28
  Keeling Curve, 20
  overabundance is the danger of,
    21–22
  permits, emission, 55–56, 58
  storage capacity, 29, 41, 46, 49–50
  temperature determinant, 17
  thresholds, 24
  See also Sky Trust
Children, educational programming
  for, 38
Children and Sky Trust, 65
Chlorofluorocarbons (CFCs), 19
Citizen ownership, Alaska-style, 50–53,
  64, 127–29
Civic institution, Sky Trust as a, 62–63
Climate change, 3, 74–75
Coal-burning power plants, 7, 19–20
Coase, Ronald, 43–44, 92
Code, installing a new economic, 131

Common assets, 99–100, 102
Common lands, 47
Commons, the new:
  biodiversity, 110–13
  creating, 122–23
  democracy, 116–17
  overview, 105–7
  ownership of the sky, 55
  quietude, 113–16
  sectors of the new economy, 128
  societal assets, 107–10
  statement, a single annual, 119,
    120–21
  stock market, 117–18, 120
  summary, 122–23
  See also Selling the sky; Sky Trust
Commons, tragedy of the, 35
Commons and the state, a confusion
  between the, 53–55
Communism, 106
Computer models, 41, 73, 76
Congress, U.S., 9, 37–38, 42
Constitution, U.S., 48
Coral reefs, 22
Corporate ownership of the sky, 49
Corporation for Enterprise
  Development (CFED), 11, 62, 65
Costanza, Robert, 39
Cost of goods sold, 89–92
Creative destruction, 74

Daily, Gretchen, 40
Dales, John, 34–35
Daly, Herman, 82, 83–84
DDT, 22
Declaration of Independence, 48
Democracy, 116–17
Derivatives, 55
Developing countries, 46
Development and the Environment,
  83–84
Diamonds and water paradox, 28
Dirksen, Everett, 38–39

Disasters, natural, 22
Dividends to ourselves, paying, 2–3,
    51–53. *See also* Commons, the
    new; Sky Trust
Dole, Bob, 38, 39
Doomsayers, 25
Dot-com IPOs, 109, 117
DRI/McGraw-Hill, 41
Droughts, 22
DuPont, 19

"Economic Possibilities for our
    Grandchildren" (Keynes), 130
Economists, thought experiments for:
    assumptions of conventional
        economics, 80–81
    dark side, where's the, 101–3
    money pipes, 97–100
    overview, 79–80
    pay-as-you-go, 91–93
    sinks are scarce, imagine waste,
        81–85
    summary, 100–101
Economy, the human economy as a
    subsystem of a larger natural,
    82–84
Ecosystem services, value of, 39–40
Edison, Thomas, 18
Ehrlich, Paul, 25
Einstein, Albert, 79
Electric utilities, 78
Elements recycled by the sky, 17
Energy Information
    Administration/Agency, 41, 76
Energy providers and subsidies, 7, 91
Engines, 18
English law, 47, 53–54
Entitlements, 44
Ethyl Corporation, 19
Exchange value, 28, 34, 41
Exhausts, the sky absorbs and moves,
    17, 18
Externalities, 85–93

Extinctions of species, 111–12
Exxon, 85

Fairness Doctrine, 38
Families aided by Sky Trust, 65
Farming, 111
Federal ownership of carbon
    absorption capacity, 49–50
Federal Reserve, 81
Federal Reserve Act of 1913, 72
Feedback loops, 23, 84–85
Financial instruments, 55
Fisheries, 50
Floods, 22
Ford, Gerald, 38–39
Forest Service, U.S., 54
Fossil fuel combustion, 4, 26, 55, 76, 91
Freshwater replenished by the sky, 16
Friedman, Milton, 43
Friedman, Robert, 11
Frigidaire, 19
Frissell, Christopher, 112

Gaffney, Mason, 44
Galbraith, John K., 81, 127
Gasoline, 19, 76, 90
General Motors, 19
*General Theory of Employment, Interests
    and Money, The* (Keynes), 129–30
Gentility, getting from greed to, 130
Genuine Progress Indicator (GPI),
    87–88
Global warming, 3, 30
Gore, Al, Jr., 22
Government:
    boundaries, setting, 11
    climate change, assessment of, 3
    commons and the state, a
        confusion between the, 53–55
    federal ownership of carbon
        absorption capacity, 49–50
    people creating government for
        their own purposes, 48

property rights, 35, 92
Governor for the human economy, 84
Gradualism and Sky Trust, 75
Greed to gentility, getting from, 130
Greenhouse effect/gases, 3, 17–18. *See also* Carbon dioxide
Greentapping, 8
Gross domestic product (GDP), 76–78, 85–86, 88, 95

Habitat occupation, 111–13
Haddock, Doris, 116
Hammond, Jay, 50
Happiness, multiple paths to, 93–97
Hardin, Garrett, 35
Harvard University, 6
Havens, John, 98
Homestead Act of 1862, 72
Hurricanes, 22

Illth, 86–88, 91, 93
Incentives driving capitalism, 129
Income, property, 96–97, 102
Income, unearned, 110
Income tax, 11
Individual Indian Money Trusts, 54
Inheritance, individual, 1–2, 5–6, 98–99
Inheritance, shared biological, 1
Inheritance, social, 107–10
Inner needs, 95
Insurance companies, 22
Intergovernmental Panel on Climate Change, 27–28
Interior Department, U.S., 54
Internal combustion engine, 18
Internet, the, xiv, 109, 116, 117
Intragenerational pipes, 99–100
Intrinsic value, 34, 41
Inventions that changed the sky, 18–19

Invisible hand, Adam Smith's, 108, 125
Ionosphere, 15

Japan, 66
Journal of Law and Economics, 43, 44

Keeling Curve, 20
Keynes, John M., 79, 129–30, 132
Kyoto Protocol, 66

Lake Erie, 22
Land, end of the era of free, 30
Lands, common, 47
Land speculation, 108
Lasn, Kalle, 114
Leaded gas, 19
Legislation:
    Federal Reserve Act of 1913, 72
    Homestead Act of 1862, 72
    Radio Act of 1927, 117
    Social Security Act of 1935, 72
Licensing system for broadcast frequencies, 37–38
Limits to Growth (Malthus), 24–25
Lincoln, Abraham, 48
Liquidity, 118, 120
Load line, 27–28
Locke, John, 47–48
Logging, 54
Los Angeles, Calif., 19, 22
Lovins, Amory, 77–78

Macroeconomic effects of a Sky Trust, 77–78
Madison, James, 48
Magna Carta, 47
Malthus, Thomas, 24
Marconi, Guglielmo, 37
Marginal utility of more stuff, 95
Market prices for using our inherited

assets, charging, 2–3. *See also*
    Commons, the new; Sky Trust
Markets and intrinsic value, 34
Maslow, Abraham, 94
McCain, John, 38, 39
Mesa Refuge, xii–xiii
Mesosphere, 15
Meteors, the sky shielding us from, 16
Midgely, Thomas, Jr., 19
Money pipes, 97–100, 129
Monopoly, 98, 101
Mutual funds, 59

Narain, Sunita, 46
Native Americans, 54
Nature, 39
Needs, hierarchy of, 94–95
Negative feedback loops, 23
Negative marginal return/utility,
    88–89
New Deal, mid-twenty-first-century,
    122
Nitrogen, 17
Nixon, Richard, 130
Noise levels, exposure to high, 114
Nuclear energy/power, 7, 91
Numbers, predictive vs. descriptive, 73
Nutrients recycled by the sky, 17

Oil issues, 7, 19, 51–53, 76, 90
OPEC, 64
Optimists, 25
Ownership of the sky:
    Alaska-style citizen ownership,
      50–53
    commons and the state, a
      confusion between the, 53–55
    Constitution, U.S., 48
    English law, 47
    overview, 45–46
    Roman law, 46

three candidates, 49–50
twenty-first century common
    ownership, 55
Oxygen, 17, 18
Ozone, 15, 18, 19

Pacific islands and rising seas, 22
Pain sharing and Sky Trust, 73–78
Pay-as-you-go, 90, 91–93
Permits, emission, 36, 41, 55–56, 58
Perverse feedback loops, 23, 84–85
Pigou, Arthur, 42, 92
Plimsoll line, Samuel Plimsoll and the,
    27–28, 92
Popoff, Frank, 33, 40–41, 92
Population growth, 111–13
Poverty:
    property rights, 11
    Sky Trust, 64
    wealth, unequal distribution of,
      81, 109–10
Precautionary principle, 26
Prices as measure of scarcity, 25
Private assets, 99–100
Privatization, 106
Products, developing new, 61–62
Profits, 10, 92
Property income, 96–97, 102
Property rights:
    cap-and-trade systems, 34–36
    Coase, Ronald, 43–44
    government, 35, 92
    initial, 44
    scarcity rent, 29
    subsidies, 91
Public trust doctrine, 47

Quietude, 113–16

Radioactive wastes, 26
Radio Act of 1927, 117

Radio signals, 17, 37
Reagan, Ronald, 7
Recycling machine, Sky Trust as a
    scarcity rent, 63–64
Redefining Progress, 10–11, 42, 62,
    86–87
Refrigerants, 19
Religion and the sky, 15
Religious justification for Alaska-style
    citizen ownership, 53
Res communes, 46, 47, 105
Res nullius, 46
Resources for the Future, 62
Res privatae, 46
Res publicae, 46, 47
Retirement, 90
Revelle, Roger, 20
Ricardo, David, 29
Rio Treaty of 1992, 27
Roads, 54, 90, 112–13
Roman law, 46, 105
Rowe, Jonathan, 86
Rubin, Robert, 54
Ruskin, John, 86–87
Russia, 108

Safire, William, 39
Sarnoff, David, 37
Scale and human economy,
    83
Scarcity is wealth, 28–30
Scarcity rent:
    computer models and the worth of
        the sky, 41
    cost of goods sold, 90
    defining, 29
    governor for the human economy,
        84
    Sky Trust, 63–64, 75
    societal assets, 109
    sulfur vs. carbon, 58
Schervish, Paul, 98

Schumpeter, Joseph, 74
Scientific Revolution, 15
Seattle, Chief, 33
Securities and Exchange Commission,
    117
Self-interest of individuals and firms,
    129
Selling the sky:
    broadcast spectrum, 37–38
    cap-and-trade systems, 35–37
    overview, 33–34
    property rights, 34–35
    tax nature, why not, 41–44
    worth, how much is the sky,
        38–41
    See also Commons, the new; Sky
        Trust
Shareholders, citizen, 127–29
Shepard, Paul, 125
Shortage economies, 94, 95–96
Silence and quietude, 113–16
Silicon, 25
Simon, Julian, 25
Sinks, waste, 24–26, 81–85
Sky, the:
    functions of, 16–17
    gift, a miraculous, 18
    Intergovernmental Panel on
        Climate Change, 27–28
    intimate connection to, 14–15
    layers, five distinct, 15
    mental separation from, 14
    scarce sky, the era of, 30–31
    spacious skies, the end of, 22–26
    thinness of, 15
    what we do to, 18–21
Sky Trust:
    algorithm, the new, 72
    beginnings of, 62
    capitalism, upgrading, 126
    Certificate of Ownership, 135
    as a civic institution, 62–63

computer models, 73, 76
dividends, what will you do with
    your, 70–73
families aided by, 65
future scenario, 66–70
gradualism, 75
key features of, 133
Kyoto Protocol, 66
macroeconomic effects, 77–78
overview, 4
pain, minimizing, 73–78
payments into and receiving shares
    from, 64
poor families, 64
safety valve, 65–66
as a scarcity rent recycling
    machine, 63–64
Transition Fund, 65, 75
See also Commons, the new;
    Selling the sky
Smith, Adam, 28, 108, 125
Smog, 19
Social needs, 95
Social screening of investments, 8. See
    also Working Assets
Social Security, 90
Social Security Act of 1935, 72
Societal assets, 107–10
Solar energy, 6–7, 91
Sources, 24–25, 82
Standard Oil of New Jersey, 19
Statement, the new commons and a
    single annual, 119, 120–21
Steam engine, 18
Stock market, 59, 117–18, 120
Stratosphere, 15
Subsidies, 7, 54, 91
Sulfur, 19–20, 36–37, 58
Summers, Larry, 84
Supply and demand, 28–29, 34
Supreme Court, U.S., 47, 51–52
Surplus economies, 94, 95–96

Survival needs, 94–95
Systemic solutions, 10–11, 92, 130–31
Systems, stresses/feedback
    loops/thresholds and, 23–24

Taxes:
    capital gains, 110
    energy providers, 7, 91
    fisheries, 50
    forests, the destruction of the, 54
    income, 11
    nature, why not tax, 41–44
    pollution control using, 41–44
    road building, 90
    shifting, tax, 11
    Sky Trust, 70–71
Telephone service, Working Assets', 9
Tenth Amendment, 48
Thermosphere, 15
Thierer, Adam, 39
Think tanks, 10–12, 62
Thresholds, 24
Time, relationship between happiness
    and, 96
Torres, Gerald, 47
Tragedy of the commons, 35
Transaction costs, 43, 92
Transition Fund, Sky Trust's, 65, 75
Transparency, 63
Treasury Department, U.S., 11, 54
Trombulak, Stephen, 112
Troposphere, 15
Trust funds, 131
Trusts, common asset, 58, 120–22,
    128, 131. See also Sky Trust
Turner, Frederick J., 30

Ultraviolet rays, 16, 18, 19
Unearned income, 110
Unemployment, 129–30
Upstream permits, 58
Uranium, 91

Utility, 88–89, 93, 95

Value, intrinsic, 34
Value in use vs. value in exchange, 28
Virtuous feedback loops, 23
Visa Card, Working Assets', 9
Vonnegut, Kurt, 125

Warming, global, 3, 30
Wastes, where do we put our. *See*
    Sinks, waste
Water and diamonds paradox, 28
Water replenished by the sky, 16
Watt, James, 18

Wealth, scarcity is, 28–30
Wealth, unequal distribution of, 81,
    109–10
Westinghouse, George, 37
White, E. B., 105
Wilson, Edward O., 111
Wind, 17
Wolff, Edward N., 81
Working Assets, 7–10, 58, 91–92, 118
World Bank, 83–84
World War II, 78

Zobel, Penny, 51
Zobel, Ron, 51